The Bakke Case
Quotas in College Admissions

Susan Banfield

Landmark Supreme Court Cases

Enslow Publishers, Inc.

44 Fadem Road	PO Box 38
Box 699	Aldershot
Springfield, NJ 07081	Hants GU12 6BP
USA	UK

1
AFD-620 7
1285590

344.0798
B

Copyright © 1998 by Susan Banfield

All rights reserved.

No part of this book may be reprinted by any means
without the written permission of the publisher.

Library of Congress Cataloging-in-Publication Data

Banfield, Susan.
    The Bakke case: quotas in college admissions / Susan Banfield.
        p. cm. — (Landmark Supreme Court cases)
    Includes bibliographical references and index.
    Summary: Provides background and discussion of the case brought
by a white male student who challenged the affirmative action policy
used in admitting students to the University of California medical school.
    ISBN 0-89490-968-1
    1. Bakke, Allan Paul—Trials, litigation, etc.—Juvenile
literature. 2. University of California, Berkeley—Trials,
litigation, etc.—Juvenile literature. 3. Discrimination in medical
education—Law and legislation—California—Juvenile literature.
4. Medical colleges—California—Admission—Juvenile literature.
[1. Bakke, Allan Paul—Trials, litigation, etc. 2. Discrimination in
education. 3. Affirmative action programs.] I. Title. II. Series.
    KF228.B34B36   1998
    344.73'0798—DC21   97-21309
                                                            CIP
                                                             AC

Printed in the United States of America

10 9 8 7 6 5 4 3 2 1

Photo Credits: Connecticut Children's Medical Center, p. 50; New York Police Department, p. 27; Reproduced from the Collections of the Library of Congress, pp. 10, 35, 38, 76, 84, 94, 98; *San Francisco Examiner,* p. 7; San Francisco Fire Department, p. 102; *The Seattle Times,* p. 53; University of California, Davis, p. 59; Yale University Library, Manuscripts and Archives, p. 16.

Cover Photo: University of California, Davis.

Contents

1

The Tables are Turned

Long before Allan Bakke brought his case, *Regents of the University of California* v. *Allan Bakke,* also referred to as the *Bakke* case, to the United States Supreme Court, the Court delivered one of its most important decisions ever. In the case of *Brown* v. *Board of Education* in 1954, the Court ruled that "separate but equal" educational facilities were inherently unequal and therefore unconstitutional.[1] The Court outlawed segregation—the separation of the races—in public schools. In spite of the sweeping implications of the *Brown* decision, change came slowly to the segregated schools of the nation's southern states. Although the Court ordered schools to desegregate and institute a policy of mixed-race classrooms, the Justices realized that tremendous changes would have to be made in order to comply with the order. Therefore they did not set an exact date by which school systems would have to be in full compliance. As a result, many schools made only token efforts to desegregate. Years after the landmark 1954 decision, many schools were still all or nearly all-white or all-black. By 1964, ten years after *Brown,* only 2.3 percent of African Americans in the South were enrolled in integrated, mixed-race schools.[2]

One young man who noticed no immediate effects from the *Brown* decision was Allan Bakke. The fair-haired, fair-skinned son of a mailman and a school teacher, both of Norwegian ancestry, young Allan attended all-white schools in Florida. Even though his years at Coral Gables High School fell largely after the *Brown* decision, Bakke, like hundreds of thousands of other young people at the time, still had the experience of all-white sports teams, clubs, and classes.

Allan Bakke went on to attend college in his parents' home state of Minnesota, where he was an outstanding student. He earned a degree in engineering from the University of Minnesota with nearly straight A's. Bakke then went on to serve four years in the Marine Corps, including service in Vietnam. His record was admirable: he left the Marines in 1967 as a captain. Once out of the service, he took a job as an aerospace engineer with the National Aeronautics and

Space Administration (NASA) at the Ames Research Center in the San Francisco Bay area. He settled in a San Francisco suburb with his wife and started a family.

Meanwhile, many African Americans of Bakke's generation were not faring nearly so well. Despite the good intentions of the *Brown* decision, very little had changed for many African Americans. Many still attended poor-quality, segregated schools, and faced discrimination in many other aspects of their lives.

In the late 1950s and early 1960s, many African Americans began to take action to correct these injustices. Both black and white citizens staged sit-ins and held protest marches. Sit-ins and marches provide a means of public protest against policies that people

Allan Bakke talks to a group of reporters and photographers. Bakke challenged the use of quotas at the University of California-Davis as a way to select students who would diversify the campus.

dislike. In a sit-in, the protesters sit in a public place, often blocking traffic, and refuse to leave. In 1964 the federal government passed the Civil Rights Act. This forbade discrimination in public facilities, in education, and in employment.[3]

Yet, despite the rulings of the Supreme Court and the intent of the government, schools seemed especially slow to desegregate. In 1964 a group of parents from Charlotte, North Carolina, filed suit. The vast majority of black students in the Charlotte-Mecklenburg school system still attended all-black schools. In 1969, federal judge James McMillan ordered that the system's schools be completely desegregated by the fall of 1970. If that meant that some students would have to be bused to white schools, then they would have to be bused, Judge McMillan maintained. The federal court decision was appealed to the United States Supreme Court, but, in *Swann* v. *Charlotte-Mecklenburg Board of Education,* the nation's highest court voted unanimously to uphold McMillan's initial ruling.[4]

The use of busing and other measures to achieve racially-mixed student bodies represented a new precedent in public affairs. It reinforced the notion that concrete measures were needed in order to correct and make up for years of discrimination. Soon many private colleges, universities, and places of employment were establishing "equal opportunity" and "equal employment opportunity" programs. These programs came to be called "affirmative action" programs. This term refers to policies designed to provide limited kinds of preferential treatment for people from certain racial, ethnic, and social groups that have been the victims of long-term discrimination.[5] In the United States, the people most often served by these programs are women, African Americans, Native Americans, Hispanic Americans, people with disabilities, and Vietnam War veterans.

A fairly typical such program was instituted at the University of California Medical School in Davis, California (U.C. Davis). In 1968 the Association of American Medical Colleges had the following recommendation: "Medical schools must admit increased numbers of students from geographical areas, economic backgrounds and ethnic groups that are now inadequately represented."[6]

The U.C. Davis faculty responded by creating a task force. Its purpose was to recruit students from underrepresented backgrounds and groups. The task force was to fill 16 percent of the one hundred places in each entering class—in other words find sixteen students. During the period from 1970 to 1974, the task force admitted thirty-three Mexican Americans,

9

twenty-six African Americans, one Native American, and twelve Asian Americans.

Meanwhile, Allan Bakke had begun to pursue a dream that had been born in him while serving in Vietnam. More than anything, he decided, he wanted to become a doctor. He worked hard to make his dream a reality: he took the necessary premed courses at night school, took the required Medical College Admissions Test (MCAT), and in 1972, began applying to medical schools. Bakke's grades and test scores were very good. His undergraduate grade point average had been 3.51

In some places, busing is used in an effort to desegregate schools. Some people feel that busing is unjust because often a student will have to be bused away from the school closest to where he or she lives.

out of a possible 4.0. On the MCAT he scored in the 97th percentile in scientific knowledge and in the 96th percentile in verbal ability. He also did well in interviews. One interviewer wrote of him: "He is a pleasant, mature person. . .a very desirable applicant to this medical school."[7] Yet Bakke was still far from being assured a spot in medical school. At a school such as Davis, for example, nearly twenty-five hundred applicants were competing for one hundred available places. In addition, Bakke's age would be sure to work against him. He was thirty-three years old, which at some schools automatically disqualified him. Medical schools frequently viewed an expensive medical education as a kind of investment. Since an older student would practice medicine perhaps ten years less than someone just out of college, he or she might be considered a poor investment of the school's resources.

Bakke was aware of the handicap his age presented, and he knew the process could be difficult and frequently dismaying. He was rejected at all twelve schools to which he applied in 1972–1973. Several schools cited his age as the reason. This Bakke had been prepared for. What he found harder to swallow was the fact that at one of those schools, U.C. Davis, minority applicants with lower MCAT scores and grade point averages than his had been admitted by the task force.

11

(One of the assistant deans at Davis, Peter Storandt, was sympathetic to Bakke and had provided him with this information when Bakke questioned him about his rejection.)

Much had changed in the twenty years since young Allan Bakke had attended all-white schools in Florida. Now he seemed to find himself on the opposite side of the fence raised by racial discrimination. Bakke wrote an angry letter to officials at U.C. Davis. "Applicants chosen to be our doctors should be those presenting the best qualifications, both academic and personal," he stated. He then went on to point out the following:

> Most are selected according to this standard, but I am convinced that a significant fraction of every current medical class is judged by a separate criterion. I am referring to quotas, open or covert, for racial minorities. Medicine needs the ablest and most dedicated [people] in order to meet future health care needs. I realize that the rationale for these quotas is that they attempt to atone for past racial discrimination. But instituting a new racial bias, in favor of minorities, is not a just solution.[8]

Six months later, Bakke applied to U.C. Davis again and was rejected a second time. What would Bakke do now? How would his actions come to help others? The process would take Bakke and his case through our court system, all the way to the highest court in the land—the United States Supreme Court.

2

Discrimination in American Life: A Long History

In August 1619, the first Africans arrived in what would one day be the United States. A ship pulled into the harbor at Jamestown, Virginia, and its captain offered to exchange for food several Africans he had captured from a Spanish ship.[1] These first African Americans were not exactly slaves, however. Nor were they regarded by the white settlers as belonging to an inferior race. The first Africans to come to North America came, for the most part, on the same footing as poor whites. They came as indentured servants.[2] Indentured servants owed their services to a master for a specified number of years, but after that time they were given their freedom. By 1624, Africans made up about 2 percent of the colony's population, numbering some twelve hundred in all.[3]

For the first forty years or so of Virginia's colonial history, black settlers lived side by side with whites on a basis of equality. They owned land, voted, held public office, and even had servants of their own—both black and white.[4] It was much the same in the other colonies. In New York, the first Africans arrived in 1626, servants of the Dutch West Indian Company. They were all granted their freedom in 1644.[5]

This period of equality was short-lived, however. By the 1660s the plantations in the southern colonies had grown tremendously in response to the rapidly expanding international market for rice and tobacco. The plantation owners' need for laborers became acute and the use of indentured servants had limitations. These men and women had to be given their freedom after a set period of time and others had to be found to take their place. Also, when servants were freed, their master was obliged to give them clothes and a small sum of money or a piece of land.[6] Instead, the plantation owners wanted slaves for life. Brief attempts were made to enslave Native Americans. But it was too easy for Native Americans, who knew the countryside, to escape.[7] The colonists then turned to Africans as a possible solution to their labor shortage. There was a precedent (previous action serving as a model) for the practice. Spanish and Portuguese settlers in South America had been using African slave-labor for over two hundred years.[8]

In the 1660s both Virginia and Maryland passed laws that made Africans slaves for life, and forbade intermarriage between blacks and whites.[9] Other colonies soon followed their lead, and the seeds of centuries of prejudice and racism were thus sown. The trade in men, women, and children from the west coast of Africa was stepped up markedly. By 1710 there were some fifty thousand Africans in the colonies. By the start of the American Revolution in 1775, there would be some five hundred thousand.[10]

During the first decades of the slave trade, back in the 1400s and 1500s, Africans and Europeans regarded one another largely as equals. The European explorers of Africa were impressed with that continent's cities and regal princes. Members of Africa's ruling class traveled to Europe to study. Africans and Europeans viewed one another as trading partners. But by the 1700s the relationship had become much more one-sided and exploitative. African ruler Mani-Congo protested. He wrote to King John III of Portugal, "It is our will that

African-American students at Yale University in the 1970s are shown here. When Africans and Europeans first came into contact with one another they treated each other as equals and trading partners. However, once the slave trade intensified it would take hundreds of years before whites and blacks would even attend the same schools.

in these kingdoms there should not be any trade in slaves or markets for slaves."[11] Too many others, however, were willing to cooperate with the Europeans.

The men and women who were sold into slavery were treated as abominably as it is possible to conceive. They were marched over land, sometimes hundreds of miles to the coast, where they were inspected like livestock, branded, and packed into ships like sardines. "They had not so much room," said one captain, "as a man in his coffin, either in length or breadth."[12] During the course of the six- to ten-week voyage, many died of disease. Quite a few tried to commit suicide; others went crazy.

Those who managed to survive the passage faced a grim existence. Most worked long and hard hours in the fields. They were increasingly scorned and ostracized by the white men and women for whom they worked. In Virginia by the late 1600s, a white person who mingled socially with blacks faced censure, official reprimand and condemnation, by fellow colonists.[13] Overseers regarded the black men and women in their charge much like animals. One remarked that breaking in a "new Negro" required "more hard Discipline than a young Spaniel."[14]

The growth of the revolutionary spirit in the colonies had some positive effect on the colonists' attitudes toward Africans. In part as a result of the widespread talk of independence, freedom, and human rights, a number of colonies passed anti-slave trade measures in the years before the American Revolution. Some individuals took steps to free their slaves. One such person was Richard Randolph. He wrote to the man managing his estate:

> I have only to say that I want not a single Negro for any other purpose than his immediate liberation. I consider every individual thus unshackled as the source of future generations, not to say nations, of freedmen.[15]

In the first years of the new nation, slavery was largely abolished in the North. One after the other, these new states passed laws granting slaves their freedom, either immediately or at least after a set number of years.[16] Abolition societies were also founded in the Mid-Atlantic and New England states. These groups worked to end the slave trade and slavery in places where it was still allowed. They also provided schooling for African Americans who had been recently freed.[17]

Still, the attitude of most white Americans toward their black neighbors was one of prejudice and often hostility. One Revolutionary War veteran of African descent, Prince Hall, said of his everyday life in Boston:

"Patience, I say; for were we not possessed of a great measure of it, we could not bear up under the daily insults we meet with in the streets. . . ."[18] As the years wore on, the northern states, where most free slaves resided, one by one took away African Americans' right to vote.[19] By the eve of the Civil War, African Americans were denied the vote in all but a few New England states.[20]

In the South, conditions were worse. Several years after the end of the Revolutionary War, Eli Whitney invented his famous cotton gin. The cotton gin, along with other advances in the manufacture of textiles, led to huge growth in the cultivation of cotton in the southern states. The demand for slaves to harvest and process the cotton also grew as a result. By the 1850s there were nearly 4 million African-American slaves in the United States.[21]

The slaves who worked the large cotton plantations led, for the most part, lives of extreme humiliation. They worked from before dawn until well into the night, under the threat of a ready whip. Former slave Charles Ball wrote:

> [I]f a slave gives offense, he is generally chastised on the spot, in the field where he is at work, as the overseer always carries a whip. . . . For stealing meat, or other provisions, or for any of the higher offenses, the

slaves are stripped, tied up by the hands—sometimes by the thumbs—and whipped at the quarter.[22]

One of the most common offenses to result in a flogging was that of impudence—overly bold disrespect for others. A master could find signs of impudence in almost anything—"in the tone of an answer; in answering at all, in not answering; in the expression of the countenance, in the motion of the head. . ." said Frederick Douglass, one of the nineteenth century's most famous escaped slaves.[23]

In addition to the whip, elaborate sets of regulations, known as "slave codes," were enacted to keep slaves ignorant and under the thumb of their white masters. Slaves were forbidden to assemble in groups larger than five. They could not leave their plantation without a pass, nor could they hold a religious meeting without a white witness present. They could not blow horns or beat drums, and they could not be taught to read.[24]

As slavery became a central feature of southern life, white southerners developed a variety of rationales defending the institution. They supported the notion of white superiority/black inferiority that formed the basis for slavery. Many whites also argued that slavery was supported by the Bible. John C. Calhoun was a prominent white southern senator of the early 1800s. He maintained that it was a dangerous error to think that all people are equally entitled to liberty.[25] One of the most widely-read supporters of slavery, George Fitzhugh of Virginia, argued that African Americans were better off as slaves.[26]

"Let Southern oppressors tremble—let their secret abettors tremble—let all the enemies of the persecuted black tremble."[27] These were the challenging words of William Lloyd Garrison, a leader of a newly-energized abolitionist movement. Its aim was to abolish, do away with, the slave trade. The movement emerged as the middle years of the nineteenth century approached. Since the time of the Revolutionary War, there had been abolitionist societies. But as slavery became more and more deeply entrenched in the South, there was a sharp increase in the number and the power of the voices that could be heard decrying its evils. Abolitionists counted among their ranks an unusual number of gifted speakers and writers, both white and black. They urged their fellow citizens not only to do away with slavery immediately, but also to end discrimination toward free African Americans.

Despite the vigorous and influential voices of the abolitionists, most Americans on the eve of the Civil War remained prejudiced toward African Americans. This was true of northerners as much as of southerners. Alexis de Tocqueville was a French historian and philosopher who traveled extensively in the United States in the 1830s. He noted that "[t]he prejudice of race appears to be stronger in the states that have abolished slavery than in those where it still exists."[28] Even Abraham Lincoln, the United States President most commonly associated with the advancement of African Americans, declared that "[t]here is a physical difference between the white and black races which I believe will forever forbid the two races living together on terms of social and political equality."[29]

It was this pervasive prejudice that enabled the country, despite the heroic efforts of the abolitionists, to enact federal laws and to make weighty legal judgments against African Americans. In 1850 Congress passed the Fugitive Slave Law. It compelled state and local officials to cooperate with the federal government in capturing runaway slaves and returning them to their owners.[30] In 1857 the United States Supreme Court handed down a decision in the *Dred Scott* case that declared slaves and their descendants to be property rather than citizens. This meant that they were not entitled to ordinary civil rights.[31]

The nation would soon be engulfed in the Civil War, a war many know as the "war to free the slaves." Only a minority of its citizens, however, supported the idea of full freedom for African Americans.

3

Government Action
Against Discrimination

In 1863 many whites in the North still harbored prejudice against their black neighbors, and many whites in the South fiercely opposed any move toward greater equality of the races. Still, that year marked a turning point in the nation's history. For in 1863, President Abraham Lincoln issued the Emancipation Proclamation. This historic document marked the entry of the federal government into the struggle against racial injustice.

> I do order and declare that all persons held as slaves within said designated States, and parts of States, are, and henceforward shall be free; and that the Executive government of the United States. . .will recognize and maintain the freedom of said persons.[1]

Unfortunately, what many people did not realize was that this document, which came in the middle of the Civil War, did not free *all* slaves—only those in certain areas of the South that were still in rebellion against the North. It also provided for the use of African Americans in the northern Army and Navy. As a result, it greatly influenced the North's victory in the Civil War.

The language of the historic document may have been dry and legal. But to the ears of the African Americans who heard it that January 1, no poetry could have sounded sweeter. When blacks and whites who had gathered around a telegraph in Boston heard the report, they jumped to their feet shouting, laughing, and crying: "It's coming! It's on the wires!" The celebration party lasted until dawn.[2] On the Sea Islands of South Carolina, Union Colonel T.W. Higginson read Lincoln's words to a group assembled at the army camp. When he was done, an old African-American man in the audience began to sing in his low, crackly voice: "My country, 'tis of thee, Sweet land of liberty, Of thee I sing." Soon every African American in the camp had joined in. "I never," Higginson said, "saw anything so electric."[3]

The Emancipation Proclamation is remembered as one of the world's greatest documents of civil liberty.

Still, it was only a small first step along the road to full equality for African Americans. If freedom for African Americans in the South was to have any meaning, the government would soon have to take more actions to protect it.

The first years after the end of the Civil War was a period called Reconstruction (1865–1877). The southern states were left largely on their own to take over again the job of governing their citizens. As many people had predicted, the newly freed southern blacks fared poorly under these first Reconstruction governments. The new southern lawmakers quickly passed laws, now known as "black codes," which were nearly as harsh as the old slave codes. The newly freed slaves were not allowed on the streets unless they could produce proof of employment. They were not allowed to carry guns, and could be whipped for trying to take part in a meeting of whites. They also could not leave the farm they worked on without permission.[4] As news of what was happening in the South spread, many northerners were horrified and cried out for the government to do something. The abolitionist members of Congress rallied, and in the following year, 1866, the Fourteenth Amendment to the Constitution, which laid the foundation for full civil and political rights for all Americans, regardless of race, was approved.

"Equal justice under law." These words are boldly inscribed on the front of the Supreme Court building in Washington, D.C., as if to symbolize all that goes on inside. To many, the words neatly sum up what the American nation is all about. The well-known phrase had its origin in the Fourteenth Amendment to the United States Constitution. Passed by Congress on June 13, 1866, and ratified by the required three quarters of the states, the amendment consisted of two parts, the first of which read as follows:

> No State shall make or enforce any law which shall abridge the privileges or immunities of citizens of the United States, nor shall any State deprive any person of life, liberty or property without due process of law, nor deny to any person within its jurisdiction the equal protection of the laws.[5]

At first, the results of the new amendment were in evidence throughout the South. African Americans started to hold public office, from the level of sheriff up to United States senator. Schools were provided for them—in several states integrated ones—and young and old flocked to attend. African Americans served on juries, gave testimony at trials, and in some instances decided cases. Socially too, there were striking changes.

After the adoption of the Fourteenth Amendment there was a brief period of time when African Americans were holding high public offices. Today this is once again the case. Shown here is Benjamin Ward, the first African-American police commissioner of New York City.

In Columbia, South Carolina, for example, blacks and whites together attended a military dress ball.[6]

The new age of equality ushered in by Reconstruction was short-lived, however. In part, this was because the courts began to find new ways to interpret the meaning of the Fourteenth Amendment. The amendment did not specifically prohibit individuals (or groups of individuals) from discriminating on the basis of race. Rather, it forbid *states* to deny anyone equal protection under the law because of their race. Therefore, in the *Civil Rights Cases of 1883,* the Supreme Court ruled that hotels, railroads, and places of public amusement could provide certain services for whites and not blacks. Hotels, railroads, and the like were owned by private individuals.

In 1896 the Court took the inequality between blacks and whites a step further. In its infamous *Plessy* v. *Ferguson* decision, it ruled that even a state could make laws for "separate but equal" facilities for blacks and whites without violating the Fourteenth Amendment. This case decided that separate railroad cars for blacks and whites on the same train were justified. The black cars, however, were markedly inferior to the white cars. The Supreme Court justified such action on the grounds that a state's police power, that is, its power and obligation to protect the public safety, took precedence over any guarantees of individual rights. The provision of separate facilities for blacks and whites was, it said, a "reasonable" use of state police powers. The Justices went still further in their interpretation of the Fourteenth Amendment. The amendment, they said, "could not have been intended to abolish distinctions based on color, or to enforce social, as distinguished from political equality, or a commingling of the two races upon terms unsatisfactory to either."[7]

In the wake of this landmark decision, the southern states passed many laws separating the two races. African Americans were required to ride in separate railroad cars, sit in separate sections in streetcars, use separate waiting rooms, orphanages, funeral homes, asylums, morgues, and cemeteries. These laws, known as Jim Crow laws, were regarded as being in full accord with the Fourteenth Amendment for over fifty years.[8]

Clearly neither the legislative nor the judicial branch of the government had the power to rid the people of prejudice so long as there was an overwhelming will to maintain it.

29

4

Attacking Discrimination in the Schools

By 1954 Americans began to show intolerance toward the racial injustices in our nation. The Supreme Court, reflecting this changing mood, overturned its 1896 interpretation of the Fourteenth Amendment, at least as it applied to public education. In accordance with *Plessy* v. *Ferguson,* the public schools in many states had long been legally segregated, or separated by race. In the late 1940s and early 1950s, African Americans began to challenge in the courts the notion of segregated education. Finally, in 1952, one case, *Brown* v. *Board of Education* made it to the United States Supreme Court. On May 17, 1954, the Court handed down its landmark decision:

Does segregation of children in public schools solely on the basis of race, even though the physical facilities and other tangible factors may be equal, deprive the children of the minority group of equal educational opportunities? We believe that it does. . . . We conclude that in the field of public education, the doctrine of separate but equal has no place. Separate educational facilities are inherently unequal. . . .[1]

Despite its importance, the *Brown* decision had a definite weakness. The Supreme Court had given only the vaguest of guidelines as to how quickly and how completely schools would have to desegregate. The Court simply said that the South should desegregate "with all deliberate speed."[2] Resistance to the decision in the South was so strong that school systems took advantage of the vague wording to completely avoid desegregating. A number of different schemes were used to postpone taking real action. Some schools adopted freedom of choice policies under which students could choose the school they went to. But numerous obstacles—a maze of red tape, buses not running between black neighborhoods and white schools, stipulations that black students could not participate in extracurricular activities with whites— prevented the vast majority of blacks from enrolling at white schools. Other school systems chose to close down their public schools rather than desegregate.

(White citizens opened private academies in churches, stores, and private homes for their children; many black children, on the other hand, were simply unable to go to school.)[3]

In some instances, when blacks did insist on their newly won right to attend formerly all-white schools, violence erupted. On September 4, 1957, a small group of eight teenagers, soon to be joined by a ninth, made its way slowly up the rise to Central High School in Little Rock, Arkansas. The young people's faces were solemn, their eyes fixed straight ahead; there was none of the carefree, joking spirit students usually show on their first day back from summer vacation.

This was no ordinary first day of school, though, and this was no ordinary group of friends. The nine teens were the first black students to attempt to enroll at formerly all-white Central High School. A recent federal court decision had required the school to desegregate. The state's governor, however, had campaigned for office on the promise that he would never allow integration in the state of Arkansas. On the eve of Central High's opening day, Governor Orville Faubus had ordered the Arkansas National Guard into Little Rock. Faubus claimed the Guardsmen were there to prevent violence. In fact they would be used to prevent the nine black teens from entering the school.

An all-white crowd had been gathering along the streets near Central High since 6:00 A.M. Some carried abusive signs. When the group of black teens walked past, the onlookers jeered and shouted obscenities. One of the girls cried.[4] Then, when that seemingly endless walk up the short block to school finally ended, the nine young people were face to face with stern-faced National Guardsmen. With their bayonets glistening in the sun, they refused to let the students enter. It took President Eisenhower's calling in of the 101st Airborne Division of the United States Army before the nine students at last made it inside the school. On September 23, seasoned paratroopers gave the students a military escort through the crowds and the taunts, and they entered Central High.

The incident at Little Rock may have been more dramatic and more highly publicized than most. But the level of resistance to desegregation involved was typical. As late as 1962, not a single black person attended desegregated public schools or colleges in Mississippi, Alabama, or South Carolina. In 1964, only a little over 2 percent of southern blacks were enrolled in desegregated schools.[5] New direction from the courts was needed. The courts might declare segregated schools unconstitutional, but could they prescribe an effective remedy?

The United States Army had to be called in to forcibly desegregate Central High School in Little Rock, Arkansas.

The first step the courts took was to be more insistent that school systems implement the *Brown* decision. In the 1965 *Bradley* v. *Richmond School Board* decision, about racial bias in teacher assignments, the Supreme Court declared: "More than a decade has passed since we directed desegregation of public school facilities 'with all deliberate speed.' Delays in desegregating school systems are no longer tolerable."[6]

By the late 1960s, the courts had become strict police officers of desegregation policy. They required school systems to design workable plans for integration. The schools also had to produce substantial, measurable results by established deadlines. In *Green* v. *County School Board of New Kent County*, the Supreme Court declared: "The burden on a school board today is to come forward with a plan that promises realistically to work, and promises realistically to work *now*."[7]

Some systems found they were able to comply with such court orders by redrawing the lines that divided school districts. They might run the new boundary lines right through the middle of a black or a white neighborhood rather than between black and white sections. Many patterns of settlement, however, did not lend themselves easily to a redistricting solution. These school systems found they could achieve desegregation quickly in only one way—by busing. Throughout the early 1970s, tens of thousands of schoolchildren in cities all across the country were bused to schools outside their neighborhood. This was done with the sole purpose of complying with the court order for full desegregation. It was a time of great tension and conflict, and very mixed results.

One of the first school systems to implement court-ordered busing was that of Charlotte-Mecklenburg, in North Carolina. As of 1960, only eight black students had been assigned to Charlotte's white schools.[8] In the fall of 1964, Mrs. Darius Swann, who was black, asked for her child to be transferred to a "desegregated," predominantly white school. Her request was refused. In January of the following year, Mrs. Swann, her husband, and twenty-four other parents filed suit. Between 1965 and 1969, more extensive desegregation was undertaken. But by 1969, fourteen thousand out of the twenty-four thousand black students in the Charlotte-Mecklenburg school system still attended all-black schools.[9]

A new judge, James B. McMillan, decided this was not good enough. It was not, he felt, what the Supreme Court had in mind.[10] He ordered total desegregation of the system's schools by the fall of 1970. In February 1970 he issued a court order stipulating that this be achieved by busing.

Thurgood Marshall was the NAACP attorney who represented the defense during the *Brown* v. *Board of Education* Supreme Court trial. Though he won the case by unanimous decision, it would take many years before schools all over the country were desegregated.

Thousands of parents came to meetings to protest the decision. Over nineteen thousand signed an antibusing petition.[11] Compliance was delayed as the decision was appealed to the United States Supreme Court. The Court, however, in a 9-0 vote in April 1971, upheld the constitutionality of Judge McMillan's order. The following fall, busing began in Charlotte.

The first year of busing was a year filled with fear, suspicion, violence, and anger. Both blacks and whites were apprehensive. Blacks often did not want to go into a new school where they would be treated as second-class citizens. They also faced the fact that positions of leadership in these schools would be closed to them.[12] Fighting was common that first year. Many students, to escape as much of the tension and conflict as they could, stopped participating in extracurricular activities. A special information center was set up just to handle calls and complaints about busing.

As early as spring 1972, however, after only six months of busing, some people were already beginning to see benefits. The children were busing's earliest supporters and did much to bring around fearful and angry parents. Said one black parent, "They [the children] were our best sellers of busing. The anxieties that parents had disappeared when kids came home feeling pretty good about themselves and what had happened in school."[13] One white parent remarked, "They gobbled up their breakfast and didn't want to be late. It was hard for a parent to counteract that."[14]

By 1978, students were once again participating in extracurricular activities and developing loyalties to their new, racially-mixed schools. Observers from around the country began to look at Charlotte's experience as a success.

In other cities, however, the results of busing were far less encouraging. A city with one of the most disappointing experiences was Boston. (It was not only southern schools that were required to bus. While schools were not legally segregated in the North, de facto segregation was common in that part of the country. The term "de facto segregation" describes situations in which African Americans are not forced by law to attend all-black schools, but in which other circumstances ensure that schools are all black or all white.)

Boston had long been a city of clearly defined neighborhoods, some black, some white. Blacks were kept out of the white neighborhoods; landlords refused to rent to them. White neighborhoods had better city services, better housing, and significantly better schools. Boston's schools were set up on a neighborhood basis, with students required to attend the schools in their neighborhood. This meant that blacks were effectively denied access to white schools and their many advantages.

In the 1960s, African Americans in Boston began to protest the de facto segregation in the city's schools. In 1965 Massachusetts passed the Racial Imbalance Act, designed to do away with de facto segregation.[15] But sentiment against integrating, bringing blacks and whites together in the schools, was strong in many neighborhoods. The Racial Imbalance Act had almost no effect. The city had a new open enrollment policy. This permitted students to transfer freely into any school in the system. Blacks who attempted to make use of the policy, however, were prevented from doing so. Black parents were not told of available places in white schools, or their requests for transfers were denied. Those few black students who did manage to transfer into white schools often were forced to sit separately or were encouraged by guidance counselors to leave.[16] Finally, black parents decided to take the matter before the courts.

On June 21, 1974, Federal Judge W. Arthur Garrity, Jr., ruled that the Boston schools were unconstitutionally segregated. He ordered that they be fully integrated within two years. Garrity also presented the school system with a plan for achieving this goal. The plan relied chiefly on busing.

The reaction of many whites was violent. On the opening day of school, hundreds of whites gathered outside of South Boston High School. They came prepared with tomatoes, bananas, beer cans, and rocks in hand to throw at the buses.[17] Even after school had begun and the buses were rolling on a regular basis, violence still occurred on a daily basis. Every day angry white crowds gathered near the schools, yelling out their protests. They threw stones at the buses and often shouted obscenities. Inside, fights between blacks and whites were a common occurrence.

Boston's schools were completely desegregated by the end of the two year period ordered by the judge. Racial tensions in the schools lasted for many years, however. Even the violence lasted. It did not taper off until the 1980s. Also, as many as two thousand white children were withdrawn from the public schools. They were sent to newly-opened segregated private schools. An untold number of white students enrolled in the city's religious schools. In all, about 10 percent of the system's students were lost to what is called "white flight."[18]

Busing was at best a controversial issue. There were real successes, such as Charlotte-Mecklenburg. Many people, however, began to question the wisdom of using such contrived means as buses and ratios to achieve integration.

5

From Civil Rights to Affirmative Action

School desegregation, busing in particular, brought with it resistance and problems. However, the momentum that had begun with *Brown* led to the start of the civil rights movement in the early and mid-1960s. Taking its lead from the schools, the nation took steps to bring equality and integration to *all* aspects of public life. In 1964 Congress passed the groundbreaking Civil Rights Act. This act of Congress forbade discrimination in all public accommodations.[1] It guaranteed that no one, on the basis of race, color, or national origin, would be excluded from participation in, or denied the benefits of, any program or activity receiving federal funds.[2] It said that employers could not fire, refuse to hire, or otherwise deny "employment opportunities" to a person because of race, color, gender, or national origin.[3] Now it seemed that equality was the law of the land, not just in the public schools, but in all walks of American life. As a result of the Civil Rights Act, some companies and public and private agencies began to take steps to achieve integration. The construction industry especially, working through the unions, began to employ more minority workers.[4] (A union is an organization of employees who work together to protect and better their wages, benefits, and working conditions.) In the late 1960s and early 1970s, federal agencies that provided benefits to employers began to require these companies to create goals and timetables in order to qualify for benefits.[5] Many states, as well as the Congress, passed "set-aside" laws. The laws required that a certain percentage of money to be distributed for public works, such as highways and bridges, be set aside for minority-owned or female-owned businesses.[6] In the field of higher education, colleges and universities began to create "special admissions" programs, such as that of the U.C. Davis task force. These programs were designed to increase the number of minority students enrolled.[7] These actions, similar to busing as a means to achieve school integration, are all examples of affirmative action.

Affirmative action refers to any measure taken to increase the total number or to improve the pay and position of minorities or females in a school, company, or organization. Imagine, for example, that a private high school is concerned that the number of Hispanic-American students it enrolls is very small compared to the total number who live in the area. The school might decide to make a special effort to send recruiters to all the local grammar schools with a large number of Hispanic-American students. It might take steps to make more scholarship money available to Hispanic-American applicants who need help with tuition. It might also decide to accept lower scores from Hispanic-American applicants on the school's entrance exam, as long as these students seemed, in general, well-qualified. These would all be examples of affirmative action.

A company might respond to complaints that it discriminated against women by adopting a policy of promoting eligible women from within before looking to hire new people from outside the company to fill managerial vacancies. It might also implement more lenient policies with respect to maternity leave or flexible working hours. This would help to make it a place in which more women would be able to work.

The company might also establish a quota for the number of women it would employ by a certain date. These, too, would all be examples of affirmative action.

By the mid-1970s, however, the country's mood on race relations had begun to change. The enthusiasm for civil rights that had previously existed was declining. Most people agreed on equality as a goal. Many, however, were beginning to question the means that should be used to achieve that goal. People were disillusioned by busing. The nation was also in an economic depression. Jobs were harder to find. People began to question the justice of such things as preferential hiring and preferential union membership for minorities.

Increasingly, affirmative action became the subject of heated debate. Strong arguments were put forth on both sides. Those who supported affirmative action argued that justice demanded that minorities be compensated for the many years of discrimination that they had suffered in the past. They also were quick to point out that if a person were not qualified to perform adequately, he or she need not be accepted for a job or a place at a university. It was not an issue of choosing unqualified minorities over qualified white people. Rather, it was an issue of choosing among equally qualified candidates.

Another common argument used in support of

affirmative action was that a diverse population, either in a student body or in the workplace, is socially beneficial to everyone. Perhaps one of the most persuasive arguments for affirmative action was that it produced results. From around the country, numerous encouraging stories could be heard of African Americans, women, and people with disabilities who had been able to achieve success in their chosen fields. These successes came, in large part, as a result of opportunities made available through affirmative action.

One such story is that of two African-American twins, Karan and Sharon Baucom. They were raised by their mother, who supported her five children sweeping floors. The girls were admitted to Missouri Medical School in the early 1970s under an affirmative action plan. They went on to become successful doctors. Said Dr. Karan Baucom: "Affirmative action may have given us extra opportunity, but where my sister and I are today is due to our family and ourselves." Her sister added: "I would have been a credit to any place that had accepted me."[8]

Diane Joyce was a widow with four young children in the early 1970s. She was employed as a clerk by the Santa Clara (California) County highway department. After working there for a while, she realized that she could do the dispatcher's job. It paid a $480-a-week salary. With four children to support, she could certainly use this money. In order to qualify for the position, Diane Joyce got the county to hire her for road crew work (the first woman ever hired by Santa Clara for such work). She spent four years flagging down traffic and shoveling hot tar. When she was able to apply she wound up as one of seven in the final pool of applicants. She began to worry, however, when she heard rumors that the supervisors had already decided to give the job to one of the male applicants. She contacted the department's affirmative action officer. He immediately intervened. He suggested that giving the dispatcher's job to Diane Joyce would help the department to meet its goals for hiring more women. Diane Joyce got the job—thanks to affirmative action. Today, there are more women working in the Santa Clara County Transportation Department than ever before—including Diane Joyce's daughter Donna.[9]

Affirmative action has also enabled thousands of men and women with disabilities to obtain meaningful employment. One of these people is David Ryan. He is partially paralyzed from the waist down, as a result of spina bifida. Spina bifida is a spinal defect present at birth. The spinal cord does not form properly. Yet today, David is a proud employee of Southern New England Telephone (SNET), where he works as an operator. He is the operator who answers when someone dials "0," as opposed to "411" operators, who look up phone numbers. SNET hired David as part of a broad-ranging commitment to helping people with disabilities. The company made an effort to hire more people with disabilities. It also made sure that all its facilities were accessible to people with disabilities. For David, the entire floor of his unit was checked to ensure that all of it would be within his reach. Today, David Ryan is a self-supporting member of his community. Not so long ago, this would not have been the case.

People who oppose affirmative action can sound just as persuasive as those who support it, however. They too have appealed to people's sense of justice. They go about it in a different way, however. They have echoed the famous statement of Supreme Court Justice John Harlan, made in 1896. He said: "Our Constitution is color-blind." Those opposed to affirmative action claim that it is the essence of the American way that people be judged as individuals rather than as members of a particular race.[10] Practical problems with affirmative action are also mentioned. Once preferential treatment is given to one group, soon everyone will want that same special treatment. When will it end? Some people have feared that once

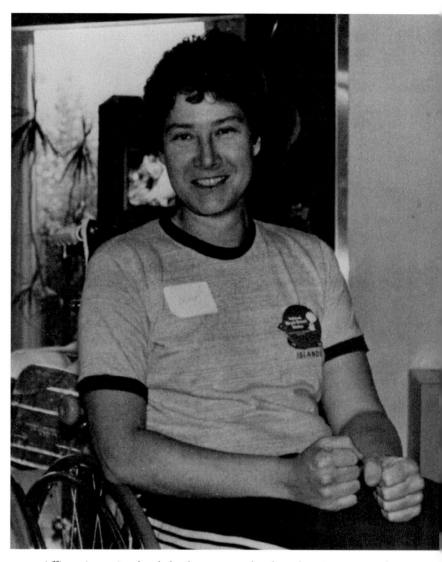

Affirmative action has helped many people who otherwise may not have had an opportunity to find employment. David Ryan works as a telephone operator in New England. His job came as a result of an affirmative action hiring program.

programs of preferential treatment were in place they would go on forever. Those against affirmative action point to the fact that there is no concrete way to determine if, or when, a debt owed for past discrimination has been paid off. Another very serious argument put forth has been that affirmative action could actually be degrading to minorities. Some people might come to judge them as unable to make it on their own merits. Thomas Sowell, an African-American economist at the University of California Los Angeles, has been one strong supporter of this view:

> What all the arguments and campaigns for quotas are really saying, loud and clear, is that *black people just don't have it,* and that they will have to be given something. . . .[Competent blacks] will be completely undermined, as black becomes synonymous. . .with incompetence, and black achievement becomes synonymous with charity or payoffs.[11]

As a result of this controversy, the 1970s saw many challenges to affirmative action in the courts. In some instances, the courts ruled in favor of affirmative action plans. In the mid-1970s, for example, the Communication Workers of America Union sued AT&T and the Equal Employment Opportunity Commission. They claimed that AT&T's affirmative action plan, which set goals and timetables for the hiring and advancement of minorities and women, was unfair to the white men in the company. In 1977 the Supreme Court ruled that the plan was acceptable. The ruling was based on the fact that AT&T had a history of past discrimination that needed to be remedied.[12] Between 1971 and 1975 federal courts issued quota orders for fire and police departments in Boston, San Francisco, Los Angeles, Baltimore, Philadelphia, and other major cities. Most of these departments had been overwhelmingly, if not completely white. The courts ordered them to achieve specified levels of minority employment by set dates.[13]

What about cases in which the institution involved had not been guilty of obvious discrimination in the past? Should such an institution be allowed to run an affirmative action program to correct general discrimination throughout society? The nation was eager to hear what the Supreme Court had to say on the matter.

In 1974 the Court got a chance to speak out on the issues raised by affirmative action. The Court heard the case of Marco DeFunis. DeFunis was a determined young white man who had done well in college. Since he lived in Seattle, he wanted very much to go to the University of Washington Law School. He was twice rejected by the school. When he found out that thirty-six out of thirty-seven minority applicants who were admitted through a special admissions program had

Before the *Bakke* case reached the Supreme Court a similar question was raised in the case of Marco DeFunis (shown here).

grade point averages and Law School Admission Test (LSAT) scores below his own, he sued.[14] DeFunis won his case in the lower court and was ordered admitted. The state supreme court later reversed that decision, however. This prompted DeFunis to take his case to the United States Supreme Court. By the time the case came before the high court, in February 1974, DeFunis was nearly through with law school. The Court declared the case moot (without legal significance), since it was no longer meaningful.[15]

Many people were disappointed with the Court's action in the *DeFunis* case. They had hoped to receive guidance from the nation's highest court on the many difficult questions involved in affirmative action. The Supreme Court could not avoid these questions indefinitely. It would only be a matter of time before Allan Bakke's case came before the Court.

6

Lower Courts Tackle the Issues

On June 29, 1974, Allan Bakke's lawyer, Reynold Colvin, filed a complaint at the local county court-house in Woodland, California, on behalf of his client. In the complaint, Colvin charged that "the sole reason [Bakke] was rejected was on account of his race." He concluded that Bakke's rights under the Fourteenth Amendment of the United States Constitution had been violated.[1]

Reynold Colvin was no stranger to affirmative action suits. In 1971 he had successfully represented a group of white school administrators who had sued the San Francisco Unified School District. They were protesting the unfairness of exempting minorities in a large-scale transfer and demotion of administrators. These actions were undertaken to save money. The ruling by the judge who heard the case condemned affirmative action in strong and direct language: "Preferential treatment under the guise of 'affirmative action' is the imposition of one form of racial discrimination in place of another."[2]

Reynold Colvin began arguing his case in the Yolo County Courthouse in Woodland. He took his presentation through the higher courts. His main arguments centered around the fact that Allan Bakke had been discriminated against because of his race. Any classification based solely on race was unconstitutional.

Colvin had to show that Bakke had been discriminated against on the basis of race. In both of the arguments he filed with the County Court and in those he made there orally during the September 27 hearing, he set out to show that the university did in fact have a quota for minority students. This was not difficult. First, in both of the years in which Bakke had applied, the task force had filled each of its sixteen allotted spaces.[3] Second, the task force claimed to be looking for applicants who were merely disadvantaged (not necessarily minorities). However over two hundred disadvantaged white students had asked to have their applications considered by the task force in 1973 and 1974. None had been admitted.[4]

Colvin also set out to prove that Bakke's chances of being admitted had been hurt by this quota system. The statistics on the undergraduate grade point averages and MCAT scores of students admitted through the task force and of those admitted through regular channels showed that two different standards of selection had been used. In one class, the average science GPA of task force students was 2.42. That of regularly admitted applicants was 3.36.[5] There were also sizable differences in the MCAT scores of the two groups.

Average Scores on MCAT		
	Task Force Students	Other Students
scientific knowledge	35th percentile	83rd percentile
verbal ability	46th percentile	81st percentile
mathematics	24th percentile	76th percentile
general information	33rd percentile	69th percentile[6]

By way of comparison, Bakke scored in the 97th percentile in scientific knowledge, in the 96th percentile in verbal ability, in the 94th percentile in mathematics, and in the 72nd percentile in general knowledge.[7] His grade point average was 3.51.[8] Colvin used this as evidence of discrimination against his client. He challenged officials at the university to prove that Bakke would not have been admitted even if the task force program had not existed. Officials at U.C. Davis were unable to do this.

Colvin took an uncompromising stand on the meaning of the Equal Protection Clause of the Fourteenth Amendment. He argued that any classification based on race—including that which he had demonstrated was used by the task force—was illegal. It did not matter what the intent of the classification was. However noble its purpose, any classification based on race was a violation of the United States Constitution. Colvin did admit that in certain cases the courts had allowed an institution to grant favor to a racial group in order to make up for having discriminated against them in the past. But he made clear that the Davis task force program could not be considered as one of these cases. The medical school had only been in existence since 1968. It had no established history of discrimination.[9]

Allan Bakke wished to attend U.C. Davis, shown here.

Colvin also put forth arguments about how affirmative action programs, such as the U.C. Davis task force, were actually damaging to minorities. Colvin claimed these programs labeled people (who were supposedly helped through such programs) as unable to meet higher standards.

Chief counsel for the university was Donald Reidhaar. Reidhaar was a quiet, traditional man. He made an eloquent statement on the university's position. Reidhaar's main point was that Bakke had ranked very low. He would not have been admitted anyway, even had there been no task force program.[10] According to the testimony of Dr. George Lowrey, who was in charge of admissions at U.C. Davis, the admissions committee looked for far more than just grades and scores. They looked for character and motivation and such qualities as imaginativeness.[11]

Reidhaar conceded that the university did have a program that considered the minority group status of applicants. But, Reidhaar pointed out, the university had the right to set admissions standards. He said:

> The special admissions program is designed to serve the legitimate needs of the Davis Medical School, the medical profession and society. This delicate and complex process of deciding which of the many qualified applicants best serve those needs must be left to

the informed judgment of those administrative officers.[12]

He pointed out that the task force considered the race or ethnic background of applicants in order to promote diversity in the student body and, later, in the medical profession itself. Another goal was to expand opportunities for medical education among those who were disadvantaged. This would help remedy what the Carnegie Commission on Higher Education called "the greatest single handicap" facing minorities—"their underrepresentation in the professions of the nation."[13] (In 1970, African Americans comprised only 2.2 percent of the nation's doctors and only a little over 1 percent of its lawyers.[14]) Reidhaar also relied on the testimony of Dr. Lowrey, to the effect that minority students helped everyone at U.C. Davis to be alert to the concerns of minority communities. The task force might also, Reidhaar said, take a candidate's race into consideration as part of its aim of expanding opportunities for disadvantaged students of all races.[15]

The judge who heard the case was F. Leslie Manker. He ruled that the Davis task force program violated the Equal Protection Clause of the Fourteenth Amendment.

> This court cannot conclude that there is any compelling or even legitimate public purpose to be

served by granting preference to minority students in admission to the medical school when to do so denies white persons an equal opportunity for admission. . . . The circle of inequality cannot be broken by shifting the inequities from one man to his neighbor.[16]

However, Manker stopped short of ordering the task force to admit Bakke. He did not think there was enough evidence to show that he would definitely have been admitted if the task force had not been in existence.

Manker delivered his judgment on March 7, 1975. It was a decision neither side could rest with. *On one hand, the university's task force program had been declared illegal. On the other hand, Allan Bakke still had not been admitted to medical school.* Lawyers for both sides began almost immediately to appeal the decision to higher courts. Within less than four months, the California Supreme Court, the highest court in the state, had agreed to hear the case. Eight months later, on March 18, 1976, Reynold Colvin and Donald Reidhaar made oral arguments before the court's seven justices. Their arguments were essentially the same as those they had made in the lower court.

The California Supreme Court had a reputation for deciding in favor of the poor, and for extending people's constitutional rights. It had been one of the first courts to raise questions about the issue of gender discrimination. It had ruled against the death penalty before the United States Supreme Court did so. The justice who would write the majority opinion for the California Supreme Court in the *Bakke* case was Stanley Mosk. He had done much in California to advance the cause of civil rights for African Americans.

With *Bakke,* however, the California Supreme Court seemed to do an about-face. Mosk, in fact, was denounced as a traitor by some of his friends from the civil rights movement. The judgment that Mosk wrote and the court delivered upheld the lower court ruling. It supported the notion that the task force program was illegal. It also went further—it ordered that Bakke be admitted to the medical school. Mosk wrote:

> We conclude that the program, as administered by the University, violates the constitutional rights of non-minority applicants because it affords preference on the basis of race to persons who, by the University's own standards, are not as qualified for the study of medicine as non-minority applicants denied admission.[17]

Mosk also quoted a powerful passage from the dissenting opinion that Supreme Court Justice William Douglas wrote in the *DeFunis* case:

> The Equal Protection Clause commands the elimination of racial barriers, not their creation in order to satisfy our theory as to how society ought to be organized. The purpose of the University of Washington

cannot be to produce black lawyers for blacks, Polish lawyers for Poles, Jewish lawyers for Jews, Irish lawyers for Irish. It should be to produce good lawyers for Americans. . . .[18]

In reaching their decision, the justices had wrestled at length with the difficult question of how to interpret the Fourteenth Amendment. They were not content, as Colvin had been, simply to assert that it forbade all use of racial classifications.

Laws, by their nature, involve unequal treatment of groups and individuals. They say, for example, that young people over a certain age have certain rights and responsibilities, such as driving a car, that young people under the set age do not have. The question that must be addressed by a court considering a certain law or a situation whose legality is in question is this: Is there is a legitimate purpose for the unequal treatment that the law or the situation prescribes? Is there, for example, a legitimate reason for giving sixteen-year-olds the right to drive, but not fourteen-year-olds? Addressing this question is known as submitting the law or situation to the "rational basis test." On the surface, a law setting a legal age for driving a car would seem to discriminate against anyone below that age. However, there is a legitimate purpose—that is, a *rational basis*—for such laws. In the case of laws setting a minimum legal age for driving, the purpose is to keep people not old enough to have good judgment off the roads. The "rational basis test" is the lowest level of scrutiny that courts apply to laws that categorize people into groups.

Courts may also review laws under what is called "intermediate scrutiny" or under what is called "strict scrutiny." When using the intermediate scrutiny standard, any good reason for a law is enough to justify it. When using the strict scrutiny standard, however, it must be proved not only that there is a good reason for the law in question, but also that the government has a compelling reason to enact the law—that there are no other ways in which its goals might be achieved.

Most laws or situations are subjected only to rational basis, minimal, or intermediate scrutiny. But historically, any law that involves basic constitutional rights, such as the right to vote or to a fair trial, must be subjected to strict scrutiny. The reason for this is that a state must have a compelling reason for denying a person such basic rights. Additionally, most laws or situations that single out one group of people for less favorable treatment than others would normally be subjected to strict scrutiny. This is to ensure that the majority does not oppress an unpopular minority.

If the task force program were subjected only to the minimal scrutiny test, it would be found perfectly legitimate. This could be based on any of the often-cited reasons for its existence. Creating a more diverse student body, providing more doctors for minority neighborhoods, and remedying the effects of past discrimination would all be judged good reasons. But Mosk argued that the task force should be subjected to strict scrutiny. He found that it did not pass that test. There were other ways, he pointed out, by which the university could have met its goals of integration and providing for doctors for minority communities. It could, for example, have instituted programs to provide remedial schooling (schooling designed to make up for deficiencies in a person's prior education) for disadvantaged students interested in a medical career. It could have expanded its enrollment across the board. It could have employed more flexible admissions standards that relied less heavily on grades and test scores for everyone.

One justice, Matthew Tobriner, dissented from the majority opinion and argument. Tobriner asserted that the strict scrutiny test should *not* apply to the task force program. His reasoning was that harmful and benign (harmless) racial classifications should be considered differently. The task force program, because it was intended to benefit minorities, could be considered as an example of the benign use of racial classification.

Due to this, it is not subject to strict scrutiny. "It is anomalous [inconsistent]," he wrote, "that the Fourteenth Amendment that served as the basis for the requirement that elementary and secondary schools be *compelled* to integrate should now be turned around to *forbid* graduate schools from voluntarily seeking that very objective."[19]

Between them, Mosk and Tobriner had begun to explore the complexities of the deceptively simple concept of "equal justice under law." This is the basic idea behind the Equal Protection Clause of the Fourteenth Amendment. Despite their long and careful arguments, however, theirs would not be the final word on the matter.

The university had lost its case at the California Supreme Court level. The court had ruled that Bakke should be admitted. It also ruled that the task force program was illegal. In mid-November, 1976, less than a month after the California Supreme Court had handed down its decision, the University of California moved to appeal the case to the United States Supreme Court. On February 22, 1977, the Supreme Court agreed to hear the case.

7

Arguments Before the Supreme Court

The date was October 12, 1977, and people had been camping out in front of the Supreme Court building since the previous afternoon. The event that had attracted the crowds was the argument of the *Bakke* case. In fact, so many spectators had come to see the lawyers present their arguments that Court officials had to rotate some spectators through the courtroom, limiting their participation time to three minutes.[1] "Not since the assassination of Martin Luther King, Jr., [1968] has this country engaged in as much soul searching about its race relations as has been triggered by *Bakke*," declared an editorial in that month's issue of *Change*, a journal of higher education.[2]

In fact, the excitement about the case had been building for months. Normally, before a case is heard by a judge, the lawyers for both the plaintiff or prosecution (the side that first institutes legal proceedings against someone in court) and the defense (the side being sued or accused) file briefs. These are explanations of how each side interprets the law that applies to the case. When the Supreme Court announces it will hear a case, in addition to the briefs from the attorneys for the two sides, it also allows other parties who have an interest to file briefs. These are called *amicus curiae* ("friend of the court") briefs. The *Bakke* case attracted an exceptionally high number of *amicus curiae* briefs—there were fifty-eight filed.[3]

By law, the United States government has a special position among the "friends of the court." It is allowed to file a brief in any Supreme Court case in which it has an interest and in which it would like to influence the Court. The writing of the government's *amicus curiae* brief for *Bakke* had become the focus of much controversy and national attention. President Jimmy Carter had entrusted the preparation of the brief to two prominent and respected African-American attorneys, Wade McCree, the nation's Solicitor General, and Drew Days, Assistant Attorney General. Days subsequently served as solicitor general during the first administration of President Bill Clinton. The attorney general is the nation's chief representative in legal matters and acts as a legal adviser to the president. The solicitor general, a presidential appointee, represents the executive department of the federal government before the Supreme Court. By early September, rumors had spread that the government brief would take a stand critical of the university. Both McCree and Days, after all, had made it to the top of their profession without the help of any special admissions or affirmative action programs.

President Carter's staff was alarmed. This was not what they expected. The brief would be viewed as the administration's definitive statement on affirmative action, one member of the president's staff pointed out. In order to protect the government's existing affirmative action programs, it was essential that the brief take a strong stand in favor of affirmative action.[4] It took several hastily called meetings and strained phone calls to get the two men to rework the brief to make it satisfactory to the administration.

When those lucky enough to gain admittance to the Supreme Court's October 12 session had been seated, the lawyers for the two sides took their seats at special long tables. There was a sharp rap of the gavel. The audience stood, and the nine Justices entered to take their seats at the mahogany bench. According to custom, Chief Justice Warren Burger sat in the center. The most senior Justices sat immediately at his sides. The newest Justices sat at the far ends.

The lawyer for the university was called on first to present his arguments, since the university was the plaintiff. The University of California had chosen Archibald Cox to represent it before the nation's highest court. Cox was a nationally known and respected lawyer. He had argued many cases before the Supreme Court and he was currently a professor of law at Harvard. He had been Solicitor General under President Kennedy and later served as special prosecutor during the Watergate hearings. His Harvard background (three of the Justices had also attended the school) and extensive legal experience with the government made Cox in many ways a peer of the Justices. He was at ease before them.[5]

In his opening statement Cox got right to the point. He spelled out in a few brief minutes the university's three main arguments:

1. All applicants were qualified.

2. The University had a right, in order to remedy generations of racial discrimination, to consider a person's race or ethnic background when

selecting from this large pool of qualified applicants.

3. A university's autonomy (self-direction, independence) in the selection of its students should not be taken away.

Cox continued:

This case presents a single vital question: whether a State university which is forced by limited resources to select a relatively small number of students from a much larger number of well-qualified applicants, is free, voluntarily, to take into account the fact that a qualified applicant is black, Chicano, Asian or Native American in order to increase the number of qualified members of those minority groups trained for the educated professions and participating in them, professions from which minorities were long excluded because of generations of pervasive racial discrimination.[6]

Cox underscored the point that admissions officers at medical schools must select from among many qualified applicants. "The number of qualified applicants from the nation's professional schools is vastly greater than the number of places available," he said.[7] He cited statistics to support this assertion, including the fact that in 1974 there were thirty-seven applicants for every available place at Davis.[8]

When discussing the great need to remedy generations of past discrimination, Cox touched on the important question of how that was to be accomplished. It could not be done, he said, without taking into account the race of applicants. "There is no racially blind method of selection which will enroll today more than a trickle of minority students in the nation's colleges and professions."[9] When the Justices questioned him about the university's use of racial quotas to achieve its ends, Cox replied that although Davis had used a quota, "it was not stigmatizing . . . in any way."[10]

Cox then proceeded to address directly the constitutionality of the task force program. The United States Constitution did not mandate that such a selection process be carried out without consideration of race, he said:

> The Fourteenth Amendment does not outlaw race-conscious programs where there is no invidious [discriminatory] purpose or intent; or where they are aimed at offsetting the consequences of our long tragic history of discrimination, and achieving greater racial equity.[11]

In his presentation, Cox especially stressed the issue of university autonomy—a school's freedom to select its own students. No one would question, for example, a medical school trying to help alleviate the shortage of doctors in rural areas. They would be justified in recruiting students from rural areas who planned to return there as general practitioners.

This line of argument inadvertently provided a few moments of comic relief in the proceedings. One of the Justices asked Cox if the use of the task force program to pursue the university's aims of increasing the number of minorities at Davis and in the medical profession was like the common practice by many schools of using athletic scholarships to improve their teams' athletic achievement. "It's the aim of most institutions, isn't it [to have athletic prowess]?" one of the Justices asked.

"Well, I come from Harvard, sir," Cox replied. "I don't know if it's our aim, but we don't do very well."[12] The Court erupted in laughter. The many Harvard graduates present enjoyed an insiders' joke about the poor performance of their school's sports teams.

Mr. Cox ended with a plea for dealing realistically with the issue of race.

> If we are talking about realities, race is a fact; it is something that all kinds of social feelings, contacts, a vision of one's opportunity, is related to. And if one is going to meaningfully direct these programs in social objectives, it is simply stultifying [foolish] to disregard a reality that we hope will stop having significance in these areas, and which will have more—and which we have a chance of depriving of its present unfortunate significance if these programs are permitted to continue and succeed.[13]

Mr. Cox's presentation was followed, not by that of Bakke's lawyer, but by arguments from a lawyer for the

United States government. This is standard practice in Supreme Court cases. Under federal law the government has a right to try to influence the Court. It could do this not only by filing briefs, but also by appearing before the Justices when cases were presented. The two people who handle this responsibility for the government are the Attorney General and the Solicitor General.

Solicitor General Wade McCree presented the government's view of the *Bakke* case. McCree supported the university and endorsed its task force program. His arguments, however, were different from Cox's. He first stressed the pervasive nature of discrimination in the United States. It was such that everyone had a responsibility to do what they could to remedy it. "To be blind to race today is to be blind to reality," McCree remarked, quoting former Solicitor General Robert Bork.[14]

Also, he pointed out, the argument that only institutions with a history of discrimination should take steps to remedy past discrimination made no sense. "We are a nation without barriers to travel,"[15] McCree pointed out. Students applied to U.C. Davis from all over the country. Many of them, in the cities, towns, and counties where they were raised, had suffered

The Burger Court of the 1970s that heard the *Bakke* case is shown here.

extensively from discrimination. It was fitting that U.C. Davis was trying to do something about this.

McCree also tackled head on the question of how the Fourteenth Amendment to the Constitution should be interpreted. Some constitutional lawyers— and Supreme Court Justices—believe the Constitution should be interpreted simply by analyzing its language (and by looking at how past judges and Justices have analyzed it). People with this belief have tended to argue that the Fourteenth Amendment should protect all persons, whatever their race, against discrimination. It says, after all, that no state shall "deny *any person. . . the equal protection of the laws.*"

McCree was of a different school of thought. He was one of many who believe it is helpful to try to determine what the intent and purpose was of the men who wrote the section or amendment in question. They believe this historical approach can help people to arrive at a more accurate interpretation.

The Fourteenth Amendment was approved during the era of Reconstruction. This was a time when many people in this country were trying to do whatever they could to help the newly-freed slaves take their rightful places in society. Lawyers for the National Association for the Advancement of Colored People (NAACP) had pointed out that the same Congress that approved the

Fourteenth Amendment had also passed a number of social welfare laws. These laws were designed specifically to benefit the freed slaves.[16] Those who wrote the amendment, many argued, certainly did not intend for it to be used to prohibit programs designed to benefit African Americans.

This was the point McCree made in his conclusion: "The Fourteenth Amendment should not only require equality of treatment, but should also permit persons who were held back to be brought up to the starting line, where the opportunity for equality will be meaningful."[17]

McCree was followed at the bench by Reynold Colvin, Allan Bakke's attorney. Unlike Cox and McCree, Colvin had never before argued before the Supreme Court. He did not feel nearly as at ease there as did Archibald Cox. Colvin began by setting forth in detail the story of Allan Bakke and his quest for admission to medical school. He wanted the focus to be on his client and his client's situation, rather than on the broad implications the case might have for others. "The name of the game is not to represent Allan Bakke as a representative of a class." he said.[18] The essence of the case, as he saw it, was that "[Bakke] was excluded from [U.C. Davis] because that school had adopted a racial quota which deprived him of the opportunity for admission into the school."[19] Using a quota in such a fashion was illegal on three grounds:

1. It violated the Fourteenth Amendment.

2. It violated the Privileges & Immunities portion of the California Constitution.

3. It violated Title VI of the 1964 Civil Rights Act.

Colvin then established that the university had, in fact, used a racial quota. It did not matter, he said, that the university spoke of it as a goal.

> There are many points in the university's brief where somehow, in order to take the sting out of the word "quota" the word "goal" is used. This is not a quota, they say, but it is a goal. We find that to be a real misuse of language. . . . Here, we have a utopia where the number is first chosen, and then the number is filled regardless of the standard.[20]

He mentioned parts of Dr. Lowrey's testimony in which Lowrey had said he would never interview anyone with a grade point average (GPA) under 2.5. He also admitted, however, that he had interviewed task force candidates with GPAs as low as 2.02.

The Justices asked him about the university's assertion that everyone admitted under the task force program was fully qualified. "You do not dispute the basic finding that everybody admitted under the special program was qualified, do you?" he was asked. "We certainly do dispute it," Colvin answered.[21]

Colvin also argued the point that it was in fact a racial quota, instead of a quota of students who were simply disadvantaged. "[It] becomes a program which is designed as a racial proposition, and that is what Mr. Bakke is complaining of," he said.[22] Colvin pointed out that only minorities had ever been admitted under the task force program, even though one third of those who applied in 1974, or fifty-four, were classified as white, economically disadvantaged.[23] He also noted that the question put to candidates on the admission application to determine eligibility for consideration by the task force was "Are you a member of a minority group?" It was not, "Are you from a disadvantaged background?"[24]

It took prompting from the Justices for Colvin to offer his interpretation of the Fourteenth Amendment. One Justice said, "We are here—at least I am here—primarily to hear a constitutional argument. . . . I would like to help, I really would, on the constitutional issues. Would you address that please?"[25]

Although he might have needed prompting, Colvin was strong and unwavering in his uncompromising approach to the Equal Protection Clause. "As we look at the Fourteenth Amendment . . ." he said, "the fact of the matter is that. . .it is discrimination on the ground of race which is forbidden."[26] It was not even so much that the quota involved a number that bothered him. What he believed made the task force unconstitutional was "fundamentally. . .that race is an improper classification in this situation."[27] It is:

> not [that] it is limited to sixteen, but [that] the concept of race itself as a classification becomes in our history and our understanding an unjust and improper basis upon which to judge people. We do not believe that intelligence, that achievement, that ability are measured by skin pigmentation or by the last surname of an individual, whether or not it sounds Spanish. . . .[28]

One of the Justices asked Colvin whether he thought race could be taken into account in the admissions process so long as it was not a crucial factor, but just one factor among many. Colvin replied: "In my judgment, the use of race as a basis for admission to medical school or the exercise of other rights is an improper measure."[29]

Colvin conceded that the University did have compelling reasons for setting up a program such as the task force. But he said he believed it could be legitimate only if it admitted candidates on the basis of economic or educational disadvantage, rather than on the basis of race. "Look at people individually in terms of disadvantage," he pleaded toward the end of his presentation.[30]

> "[T]he . . . benefit of looking at the question of disadvantage," Colvin explained, "is that it meets the problem where it exists. It meets it at the point of the individual. It does not generalize. It is not true that all members of a race have exactly the same experience."[31]

Colvin had begun on an individualist note: ". . . the first thing that I ought to say to this Honorable Court is that I am Allan Bakke's lawyer and Allan Bakke is my client."[32] Right up to the end he argued the case for an interpretation of the Fourteenth Amendment that viewed people as individuals rather than as members of any class, race, or other group.

"Thank you gentlemen; the case is submitted." This was the Justices' traditional announcement that oral arguments were over.

8

A Decision, but Little Agreement

It was nearly the end of June 1978. Reporters and camera crews were camped out near the Supreme Court building. They had been there since early May, awaiting a decision in the *Bakke* case. The Supreme Court does not announce in advance when it will deliver its decision in any specific case. The press, along with the rest of nation, had to wait.

There is, however, one fairly sure way to tell the day an important decision will be handed down. On that day, some of the Justices' spouses may come to Court for the reading of the ruling. On the morning of Wednesday, June 29, Cecelia Marshall, Marjorie Brennan, Mary Ann Stewart, and Elizabeth Stevens were sighted arriving at the Court.[1] This would be the day.

Supreme Court Justice Lewis Powell is shown here. Powell gave the plurality opinion in the *Bakke* case.

At 10:00 A.M. sharp, Chief Justice Warren Burger stepped out from behind the red velvet curtains and the marshal of the court sang out the traditional call to order, "Oyez, oyez, oyez" (Hear ye, hear ye, hear ye). The Court was in session. First the Justices announced decisions in two minor cases. Then Justice Lewis Powell began to speak. "Perhaps no case in my memory has had so much media coverage. We speak today with a notable lack of unanimity. I will try to explain how we divided."[2]

This case had been far from an easy decision. It was the product of deep divisions among the nine Justices. In fact, no one opinion had received a majority of the Justices' nine votes.

- Four of the Justices (Stevens, Burger, Stewart, and Rehnquist) concluded that Bakke had been treated unlawfully under Title VI of the Civil Rights Act of 1964. They concluded that he should be admitted, as had the California Supreme Court.

- Four others (Brennan, White, Marshall, and Blackmun) concluded that the task force program *did not* violate the Fourteenth Amendment. This was a reversal of one part of the California Supreme Court decision.

- Justice Lewis Powell had voted with the first four

on the issue of Bakke's admission and with the second four on the constitutionality of affirmative action.

Because his was the swing vote in both parts of the decision, Powell wrote the opinion in the case. He wrote what is called a "plurality opinion." Such an opinion announces the judgment of the Court, but has been unable to secure the agreement of a majority of the participating Justices.

Lewis Powell was appointed to fill the seat of the late Justice Hugo Black in 1971. Powell was a thin and scholarly Virginian who had once said he would rather be a lawyer than a judge.[3] In fact, Powell had a distinguished career as a lawyer. He graduated from Harvard Law School, practiced as a partner in one of Richmond, Virginia's, oldest law firms, and served as president of the American Bar Association (ABA). When he was appointed to the bench, many people had expressed doubt that this wealthy southerner could be sensitive to the issues of poverty and race that frequently confronted the Supreme Court. However, Powell's record proved the doubters wrong. In the 1950s, when he headed up the Richmond School Board, Powell had led the city through the tensions and difficulties of court ordered school desegregation with tact and moderation. As ABA President, he had supported President Lyndon Johnson's call for free legal services for the poor. As a Supreme Court Justice, Powell had earned a reputation for finding middle ground and writing careful, thoughtful opinions in cases such as the Denver school desegregation case of 1973.[4] Among the other Justices, Powell had a reputation for hard, meticulous work. But he also had his lighter side. The Justice's eyes would light up when people began to talk about baseball. Not only would Powell rather have been a lawyer, but some speculated he might also have preferred being a first baseman to being a Supreme Court Justice.[5]

Powell's main argument was that the university had violated Title VI of the Civil Rights Act. "Racial and ethnic distinctions of *any sort* are suspect," he said.[6] Therefore they must be subject to the highest level of scrutiny. He rejected the argument that racial classifications that work against the white majority could be considered benign and thus not subject to strict scrutiny. "The concepts of majority and minority necessarily reflect temporary arrangements and political judgments."[7] Powell then proceeded to apply the strict scrutiny test (evidence both that there is a compelling reason for a law or situation, and that it is necessary) to each of the four goals the task force program claimed to serve. On each count, he found the task force lacking. Its goal of increasing the number of traditionally disfavored minorities in medical schools and in the medical profession he declared invalid. He called it "discrimination for its own sake."[8] As for increasing the number of physicians who will practice in currently underserved communities, Powell said the task force program was not needed to meet that goal. The goal of countering the effects of societal discrimination he said was too indescribable a concept. It was different from the specific, identifiable injuries due to discrimination that are often found in school desegregation or employer discrimination cases.[9] Last, he found the goal of obtaining the educational benefits that come from an ethnically diverse student body a good and reasonable goal. But Powell did not think that the task force program, set up as it was with a reliance on strict racial quotas, was necessary to meet the goal. "The diversity that furthers a compelling state interest encompasses a far broader array of qualifications and characteristics of which racial and ethnic origin is but a single though important element," he declared.[10] Powell then went on to cite the Harvard University admissions program as a model. At Harvard, he pointed out, applicants' race is considered, but in conjunction with many other factors. There are no set quotas for minorities. Also, all applicants, both white and minority, are compared with all other applicants. "In such an admissions program," Powell said of Harvard's procedure, "race or ethnic background may be deemed a 'plus' in a particular applicant's file, yet it does not insulate the individual from comparison with all other candidates."[11]

The second part of the opinion, in which Powell justified the consideration of race in university and college admissions programs, was rooted in the First Amendment. Powell had rejected the idea of remedying historic societal discrimination as a basis for allowing admissions committees to consider a candidate's race. Instead, he said that justification for such consideration was to be found in the First Amendment's aim of creating in American society an enriching exchange of ideas. "It is not too much to say that 'the nation's future depends upon leaders trained through wide exposure to the ideas and mores of students as diverse as this Nation of many peoples."[12] *Bakke had won his case at the Supreme Court level, and the university was ordered to admit him.*

Because of the emotion-charged nature of the *Bakke* case, many of the remaining eight Justices chose to speak at the June 29th session, rather than simply have their opinions appear in print. Justice John Paul Stevens, the newest member of the Court, had written the opinion for the four Justices who had supported Bakke's admission. Stevens had been a Justice only since 1975, but already had a reputation for independence. He and his three associates had chosen to base their decision on an interpretation of Title VI of the Civil Rights Act rather than to justify it on constitutional grounds. (It is common practice for the Court to avoid a constitutional issue if it can decide a case on other grounds.) Title VI, Stevens declared, "is an unusually clear, color-blind statute."[13] Section 601 of the law read in part: "No person in the United States shall, on the ground of race, color, or national origin, be excluded from participation, be denied the benefits of, or subjected to discrimination under any program or activity receiving federal financial assistance." Since the university received federal funds, and since Allan Bakke had been excluded from participation in the task force program on the basis of his race, the university's action had been illegal, Stevens concluded.

Justice William Brennan's opinion was that of the four Justices who had supported the university and its task force program. Brennan attacked those who supported color-blind interpretations of both laws and the Constitution in his opening remarks. "We cannot . . . let color blindness become a myopia which masks the reality that many 'created equal' have been treated within our lifetimes as inferior both by the law and their fellow citizens," he declared.[14]

Brennan first set out to prove that Title VI did not prohibit all race-conscious efforts to ensure that minorities received the benefits of federal programs. He said that the law had anticipated race-conscious affirmative action as one means of achieving its purpose. He cited four different Department of Health, Education and Welfare regulations. These showed that it actually required affirmative action in instances where there was evidence of past discrimination and allowed it in others.

Unlike Stevens, Brennan did not shy away from the constitutional question. He next set out to prove that the Equal Protection Clause of the Fourteenth Amendment does not mean the Constitution is color-blind. It does not prohibit all racial classifications. He argued that a case such as *Bakke,* which both Reynold Colvin and Justice Powell had said should be subjected to strict scrutiny, and which the university said required only minimal scrutiny because its purpose was benign, in fact required a test in between the two. He proposed a test used in cases of sex discrimination, in which the classification "must serve important governmental objectives and be substantially related to [but not absolutely necessary for] achievement of those objectives."[15] When subjected to this test, Brennan found that the Task Force program passed.

Brennan also took issue with Justice Powell's citing of the Harvard plan as a model. There was no real difference between the two, he said. "Any given preference that results in the exclusion of a white candidate is no more or less constitutionally acceptable than a program such as that at Davis."[16] Interestingly, statistics showed that the Harvard program produced about the same percentage of minority students as did the Davis quota system. The 1978 Harvard College class was 8.1 percent African American, 4.6 percent Hispanic American, 5.7 percent Asian American, and .4 percent Native American, a total of 18.8 percent minority.[17] The task force created classes that were 16 percent minority.

Several of the Justices who had signed Brennan's opinion felt strongly enough about the case that they also wrote opinions of their own. One of these was Harry Blackmun. To many, the impassioned statements of this Justice from Rochester, Minnesota, came as something of a surprise. Blackmun had a reputation for being a conservative, which in politics tends to mean that he favored the status quo. The conservative view of affirmative action was generally one of disapproval. Instead, Blackmun gave a moving defense of affirmative action. He compared racial preferences in admissions to the kind of preference shown in giving out athletic scholarships.

> It is somewhat ironic to have us so deeply disturbed over a program where race is an element of consciousness, and yet to be aware of the fact, as we are, that institutions of higher learning . . . have given conceded preferences up to a point to those possessed of athletic skills, to children of alumni, to the affluent who may bestow their largesse on the institution, and to those having connections with celebrities, the famous, and the powerful.[18]

Blackmun's opinion had an especially strong closing. "In order to get beyond racism," he said, "we must first take account of race. There is no other way."[19]

Thurgood Marshall, the first African-American Justice to sit on the Supreme Court, was the last to address the audience. Marshall had spent most of his legal career fighting for justice for his people. He had been named head of the legal staff of the NAACP back in 1938. From that time on he had worked tirelessly to find a peaceful, legal solution to the many injustices suffered by African Americans. In 1954 he had his first great victory. He argued the case of *Brown* v. *Board of Education of Topeka, Kansas* before the Supreme Court—and won it. But now, some twenty-five years after *Brown*, many African Americans still had not reaped the fruits of that landmark decision. "The

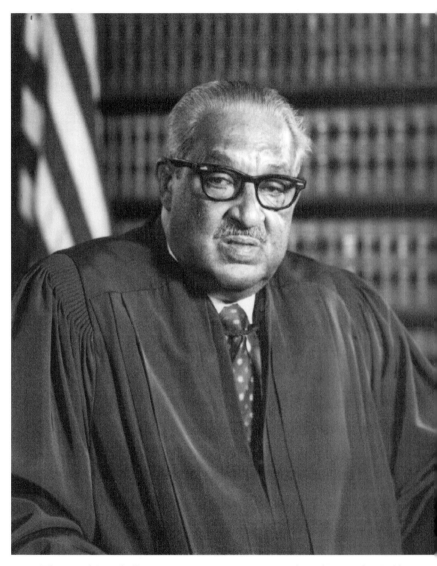

Thurgood Marshall wrote an opinion contrary to the ruling in the *Bakke* case. He was displeased with the decision and felt that affirmative action was necessary to try to combat "class-based" discrimination.

position of the Negro today in America is tragic," he said.[20] Many of the nation's best schools, especially its professional schools, were very largely white. To Marshall, the need to remedy these years of discrimination could not have been clearer.

He began the opinion by reminding people of the unique experience and history of African Americans.

> The experience of Negroes in America has been different in kind, not just in degree, from that of other ethnic groups. It is not merely the history of slavery alone but also that a whole people were marked as inferior by the law. . . . The dream of America as the great melting pot has not been realized for the Negro; because of his skin color he never even made it into the pot.[21]

Marshall then reminded his audience of the Supreme Court's role in maintaining the inferior status of African Americans. He spoke of its repeated failures to protect the rights of freed slaves after their emancipation. "It is more than a little ironic," he concluded, "that after several hundred years of class-based discrimination against Negroes, the Court is unwilling to hold that a class-based remedy for that discrimination is permissible."[22]

It was over. The Justices had finished their presentations. The Supreme Court had issued a two-part decision:

- In the first part, five Justices ruled against the medical school's special admissions program, and ordered that Allan Bakke be admitted.

- The second part of the decision stated that schools could consider race or ethnic background as *one factor* among others in determining admissions.

The decision was widely regarded as a compromise. It did not, however, help schools determine how to achieve a desired racial mix of students without using impermissible racial quotas.

There had been passionate and eloquent statements on both sides, and it seemed, at first, as though both sides had won. Throughout the case, Allan Bakke had refused to speak to anyone about the proceedings. He had vigorously guarded his privacy. On the morning after the decision, he covered his face with a newspaper as he dashed away from reporters to get to his car to go to work. But he did have his lawyers announce that he was pleased with the outcome.[23] On the other hand, a spokesman for the university declared: "I consider it a victory for the University of California."[24] Whether or not everyone had really won could be told only in time.

9

Affirmative Action
Since *Bakke*

It seemed as though the Supreme Court had given everyone a share of the victory. Some people, however, were quick to point out the flaws in this perception. Jesse Jackson, a nationally known African-American leader, pronounced the decision part of a national "move to the right."[1] (When used politically, the word "right" refers to people who would prefer to keep things the way they have been traditionally, and who view with distrust any new government intervention in people's lives.) Other African-American leaders soon echoed Jesse Jackson's distrust. They pointed out that the *Bakke* decision made affirmative action permissible but did not make it required.[2]

A group of demonstrators protest outside of the Supreme Court prior to the decision in *Regents of the University of California* v. *Allan Bakke.*

When classes began at the University of California Medical School at Davis, in the fall of 1978, Allan Bakke was greeted by demonstrators and protesters as he arrived on campus. U.C. Davis Medical School had modified its minority admissions program as a result of the Supreme Court decision. Now, each applicant would be rated according to a point system. Students would receive points for good grades, points for their MCAT scores—and would receive a set number of extra points if they were members of a minority group or were disadvantaged. But minorities were no longer assured sixteen places in each freshman class.[3] Many other schools had also revised their special admissions programs. Some had dropped minority admissions programs altogether.

Bakke's impact on higher education had pretty quickly become clear. The case had inspired a move toward more subjective, Harvard-style special admissions programs at some schools. There was a backing off from special admissions of any kind at other schools. Now people were eager to know what its impact would be on affirmative action programs in the field of employment.

In 1979, the year after the *Bakke* decision, the Supreme Court ruled in favor of a private employer's right to use affirmative action. The case was known as

United Steelworkers v. *Weber.* In Gramercy, Louisiana, African Americans made up 43 percent of the population. Yet at the local Kaiser Aluminum plant, only 5 percent of the skilled craftworkers were minorities.[4] As a result, the United Steelworkers Union had agreed with Kaiser to send the same number of white and black employees for training for the skilled positions until the percentage of minorities in skilled jobs equaled the percentage of minorities in the population at large. This would mean that blacks with less seniority than white employees would often be chosen for training. Brian Weber was a white lab technician at Kaiser who had applied for the training. He had been turned down and decided to sue. When his case reached the Supreme Court, the Justices ruled that the affirmative action plan Kaiser had set up was permissible.

In 1980, the Supreme Court ruled in favor of another affirmative action program. This one involved the federal government. The program in question was the set-aside program established by the Public Works Employment Act of 1977. According to this act, 10 percent of the money states received for public works projects such as bridges and highways was to be set aside for minority businesses. The Supreme Court, in the case of *Fullilove* v. *Klutznik,* said the program was permissible, as for many years white business owners had enjoyed an advantage over minority businesses.[5]

National attitudes toward affirmative action began to change in the early 1980s, however. The economy had worsened, and more white workers began to resent plans that would give minority workers an advantage in the competition for hard-to-find jobs. Under President Reagan, efforts to help African Americans and other minorities declined. The Department of Justice relaxed the standards it used to measure the fairness to minorities of job testing. It enforced civil rights laws less vigorously. In fact, the number of civil rights cases filed by the Department of Justice fell from 5.4 percent of all the cases it filed under President Carter to just 1.9 percent of cases in Reagan's first year.[6] A survey conducted in 1988 showed that 80 percent of whites and 50 percent of blacks thought that blacks should not "receive preference over equally qualified whites in getting into college or getting jobs."[7]

The response of the nation's courts to cases involving affirmative action in the workplace became mixed. In the early 1970s many large cities, including San Francisco, Minneapolis, Boston, Los Angeles, Baltimore, and Philadelphia, had begun to use numerical ratios when hiring police officers and fire fighters. This was done in order to increase the number of

Efforts have been made by some businesses and government agencies to integrate their staff. Shown here is the San Francisco Fire Department, First Academy Graduating Class, from 1970 (above), and 1991 (below). The 1991 class is noticeably more diverse.

minorities on their forces.[8] The courts had by and large upheld or even initiated these efforts. In 1984, however, the Supreme Court ruled in favor of a group of white Memphis fire fighters who had sued over some of that city's efforts to increase the number of African Americans on the force. In the early 1970s, only 4 percent of Memphis fire fighters had been African American. As had been done in other cities, Memphis had agreed to hire 50 percent minorities until the percentage of minorities on the force reached that of the general population—35 percent. Then, in 1980, the city had to lay off twenty-four fire fighters due to a budget cut. Under the existing seniority system, fifteen of the twenty-four would have been newly hired African Americans. The local court worked out an arrangement whereby only three blacks and twenty-one whites would be let go.[9] The white fire fighters who were laid off sued. The Supreme Court ruled in their favor. In *United Steelworkers* v. *Weber,* the Court had ruled that the need to remedy past discrimination could justify overriding a seniority system. When deciding on promotions however, the Court held that it was inappropriate to use this justification to deny an innocent employee the benefits of his seniority as applied to layoffs. In addition, *United Steelworkers* dealt with a private employer and not a city.

Gradually the Supreme Court began to impose restrictions on the use of affirmative action programs in the field of employment. In 1989, in the case of *Richmond* v. *J.A. Croson Co.,* the Court ruled that affirmative action programs of state and local governments would be subject to "strict scrutiny." They would have to be proved to serve a "compelling" (very important) interest. Richmond, Virginia, had adopted a set-aside program under which 30 percent of the money awarded by the city to each main construction contractor had to be used to hire minority subcontractors. Richmond justified the program on the grounds that it needed to correct general "societal discrimination." But, the Supreme Court ruled that, under the strict scrutiny/compelling interest test, correcting general societal discrimination was not a sufficiently good reason to adopt a race-conscious classification.[10]

Looser standards still applied in cases involving the federal government, however. In the 1990 case of *Metro Broadcasting, Inc.* v. *F.C.C.* the Supreme Court ruled that a federal agency could use a racially-based affirmative action program so long as it was substantially related to an important government interest. This was much easier to demonstrate than whether or not a program served a "compelling interest." In the *Metro Broadcasting* case, the Court upheld two Federal Communications Commission policies that gave minorities preferential treatment. Under one, applications from minorities to establish a new radio or television station would be given an advantage over applications from other people. The Court found the policies substantially related to the important government interest of promoting diversity in broadcast programs.[11]

By 1995, however, the Supreme Court had ruled that even federal affirmative action programs would be subjected to strict scrutiny. They would be required to show that they served a "compelling government interest." A number of federal laws and regulations required that most federal construction contracts contain a clause saying that a main contractor would be compensated an additional 10 percent when it subcontracted out part of its work to a business that qualified as a "Disadvantaged Business Enterprise" (DBE). If a business was owned by a member of certain minority groups, it would automatically qualify as a DBE.

Mountain Gravel & Construction Co. was the main contractor on a highway construction project for the United States Department of Transportation. Mountain took bids from subcontractors for putting in the guardrails. Adarand Constructors was the low bidder on the guardrail work. Mountain awarded the contract to Gonzales Construction Co., however. It was a minority-owned business. Adarand sued. The Supreme Court ruled in favor of Adarand. In her majority opinion in *Adarand* v. *Peña,* Justice Sandra Day O'Connor stated that henceforth:

> All racial classifications, imposed by whatever federal, state, or local governmental actor, must be analyzed by a reviewing court under strict scrutiny. In other words, such classifications are constitutional only if they are narrowly tailored measures that further compelling governmental interests.[12]

This meant that from 1995 on, in order to remain legal, any government affirmative action program would have to do the following:

1. Involve temporary measures, with a definite ending point.

2. Target actual past discrimination against a specific minority group, either by a governmental agency or by the people within the jurisdiction in question.

3. Be narrowly focused to achieve a specific result.

Programs designed simply to achieve diversity, with the possible exception of special admissions programs at state universities, would not pass the test. Nor would programs aimed at remedying general societal discrimination.

After *Adarand,* it will be harder than ever to justify affirmative action programs. Even many programs sponsored by private industries may come under question. They have often been instituted in order to comply with federal regulations which *Adarand* has now made illegal. What will be the future of affirmative action? It is hard to say.

California's Proposition 209 enacted in 1997 prohibits affirmative action hirings (with preference to race or gender) throughout the state. Challenges to this ruling are sure to follow.

Stephen Carter is an African-American law professor at Yale University. He has called himself an "affirmative action baby."[13] He freely admits he got into law school because he is African American. Carter has reflected at length on the experience of being a beneficiary of a special admissions program. He is quick to point out the negatives about such programs. Yet would he do away with them? His answer is no. He feels that "what matters most is what happens after the preference." Carter also believes, however, that "with the proper goal in mind, then, a degree of racial consciousness in college and perhaps professional school admission can plausibly be justified."[14]

Andrew Hacker is a professor of political science at Queens College in New York City. He asserts that "affirmative action is alive and well on the nation's campuses. No colleges today turn down black applicants who meet their academic criteria," he points out, adding that "virtually all schools say they would like to attract even more black students; . . . almost all mount recruiting drives."[15]

But other voices applaud the recent direction of the Supreme Court's rulings against affirmative action. Shelby Steele is an African-American professor of English at San Jose (California) State University. He says that as his children get ready to apply to colleges, it bothers him that they might have an edge in the college lottery just because they are African American. Instead of affirmative action he would rather see:

> social policies that are committed to two goals: the educational and economic development of disadvantaged people regardless of race and the eradication from our society—through close monitoring and severe sanctions—of racial, ethnic, or gender discrimination. Preferences will not get us to either of these goals.[16]

Clarence Thomas is currently the only African-American Justice on the Supreme Court. He agrees with Steele. ". . .to whatever extent we do want to give preferences to compensate those who have been unfairly deprived of certain advantages," Thomas says:

> We should do so in a manner that is just. Any

preferences given should be directly related to the obstacles that have been unfairly placed in those individuals' paths, rather than on the basis of race or gender, or on other characteristics that are often poor proxies [substitutes] for true disadvantage.[17]

The questions raised by affirmative action—What is the true nature of justice and equality? How should we turn around the effects of centuries of racial prejudice?—are among the most important questions that Americans can discuss. As the debate over affirmative action and special admissions continues, let us hope that we will all find answers that we can live with.

Questions for Discussion

1. Do you think the Constitution of the United States is color blind? Support your answer with historical examples.

2. Which do you think are more influential on a student who is a member of a minority group—the positive effects of admission to school through affirmative action or the negative effects? Support your answer.

3. What, if anything, do you think the United States owes to members of minority groups who have been subject to discrimination?

4. Do you think that school admissions, business hiring practices, and promotions should be based solely on merit? Is an attempt to make up for past discrimination a valid reason for preferential treatment? Support your answer.

5. Imagine you are a member of a particular group of people that has been subject to discrimination but never received the benefits of affirmative action programs. What, if anything, would you want the government to do for your group?

6. Do you think there should be different laws regarding special admissions programs for different types of schools? For example, should there be different standards for state universities than for private colleges?

7. Chief Justice Lewis Powell maintained that it was acceptable to consider a student's race as one factor when deciding whether or not to admit him or her to a school. Strict racial quotas, however, were unacceptable. If you were a member of a minority group who was admitted to a college under a special admissions program, would it change the way you felt about your accomplishments?

8. Do you think there should be different laws regulating the use of affirmative action programs in (1) schools, (2) industry, (3) community services such as fire and police departments? Support your answer.

9. Imagine that you were in charge of hiring the staff of a small college. What guidelines would you follow in your hiring practices? How, if at all, would an applicant's race be considered in your hiring decisions?

10. One Supreme Court Justice compared special admissions programs to admissions programs that favor applicants who are especially good at a particular sport, such as football or basketball. In what ways do you think the two situations are alike? In what ways are they different?

Chapter Notes

Chapter 1

1. 347 U.S. 483 (1954).

2. J. Harvie Wilkinson, *From Brown to Bakke: The Supreme Court & School Integration, 1954–1978* (New York: Oxford University Press, 1979), p. 65.

3. Civil Rights Act of 1964, 42 U.S.C. 1981, et. seq.

4. *Swann v. Charlotte-Mecklenburg Board of Education,* 402 U.S. 1 (1971).

5. John J. Patrick, *The Young Oxford Companion to the Supreme Court of the United States* (New York: Oxford University Press, 1994), p. 15.

6. Joel Dreyfuss and Charles Lawrence III, *The Bakke Case: The Politics of Inequality* (New York: Harcourt Brace Jovanovich & Company, 1979), p. 19.

7. Ibid., pp. 17–18.

8. Ibid., p. 14.

Chapter 2

1. Lerone Bennett, Jr., *Before the Mayflower: A History of Black America* (Chicago: Johnson Publishing Co., 1987), p. 29.

2. Ibid., pp. 34–35.

3. Ibid.

4. Ibid., pp. 35, 38.

5. Ibid., p. 41.

6. Benjamin Quarles, *The Negro in the Making of America,* rev. ed. (New York: Collier, 1969), p. 34.

7. Bennett, pp. 44–45.

8. Quarles, p. 19.

9. Bennett, p. 46.

10. Ibid., p. 47.

11. Ibid., p. 49.

12. Quarles., p. 49.

13. Bennett, p. 43.

14. Quarles, pp. 69–70.

15. Bennett, p. 69.

16. Ibid., pp. 69–70.

17. Quarles, pp. 56–57.

18. Chilton Williamson, *American Suffrage: From Property to Democracy 1760–1860* (Princeton, N.J.: Princeton University Press, 1960), p. 278.

19. Ibid.

20. Steven Lawson, *Black Ballots: Voting Rights in the South 1944–1969* (New York: Columbia University Press, 1976), p. 1.

21. John F. Bayliss, *Black Slave Narratives* (New York: Collier, 1970), p. 55.

22. Ibid.

23. Bennett, p. 109.

24. Quarles, p. 109.

25. Ibid., p. 67.

26. Ibid.

27. James H. Dormon and Robert R. Jones, *The Afro-American Experience: A Cultural History Through Emancipation* (New York: John Wiley & Sons, Inc., 1974), p. 232.

28. David Donald, *Lincoln* (New York: Simon & Schuster, 1995), p. 221.

29. Ibid.

30. Fugitive Slave Law, 1850.

31. Don E. Fehrenbacher, *The Dred Scott Case: Its Significance in American Law and Politics* (New York: Oxford University Press, 1978), p. 244.

Chapter 3

1. Emancipation Proclamation, January 1, 1863.

2. Lerone Bennett, Jr., *Before the Mayflower: A History of Black America* (Chicago: Johnson Publishing Co., 1987), p. 199.

3. Ibid., pp. 198–199.

4. Benjamin Quarles, *The Negro in the Making of America,* rev. ed. (New York: Collier, 1969), pp. 129–130.

5. United States Constitution, Amendment XIV.

6. Bennett, p. 216.

7. *Plessy* v. *Ferguson,* 163 U.S. 537 (1896).

8. Ibid., p. 268.

Chapter 4

1. 347 U.S. 483, 493 (1954).

2. Ibid.

3. J. Harvie Wilkinson, *From Brown to Bakke: The Supreme Court & School Integration, 1954–1978* (New York: Oxford University Press, 1979), pp. 83, 98–99.

4. Emma Gelders Sterne, *They Took Their Stand* (New York: Crowell-Collier Press, 1968), p. 197.

5. Wilkinson, p. 65.

6. Ibid., p. 101.

7. Ibid., p. 116.

8. Howard Maniloff, "Community Attitudes Towards a Desegregated School System," Dissertation, Teachers College, 1979, p. 42.

9. Ibid., p. 46.

10. Ibid.

11. Ibid., p. 49.

12. Ibid.

13. Ibid., p. 52.

14. Ibid., p. 80.

15. Ibid.

16. Jon Hillson, *The Battle of Boston* (New York: Pathfinder Press, 1977), p. 42.

17. Ibid., p. 23.

18. Ibid., p. 250.

Chapter 5

1. 42 U.S.C. 1981, et seq.

2. Joel Dreyfuss and Charles Lawrence III, *The Bakke Case: The Politics of Inequality* (New York: Harcourt Brace Jovanovich & Company, 1979), pp. 214–215.

3. 42 U.S.C. 2000e, et seq.

4. Geraldine Woods, *Affirmative Action* (New York: Franklin Watts Inc., 1989), pp. 58–59.

5. Ibid.

6. Ibid.

7. J. Harvie Wilkinson, *From Brown to Bakke: The Supreme Court & School Integration, 1954–1978* (New York: Oxford University Press, 1979), p. 266.

8. Richard D. Lyons, "Black Sisters: Doctors Without Fanfare," *The New York Times,* June 30, 1978, p. B-2.

9. Melvin I. Urofsky, *A Conflict of Rights: The Supreme Court and Affirmative Action* (New York: Scribner's Sons, 1991), pp. 6–14, 188.

10. Wilkinson, p. 290.

11. Ibid., p. 297.

12. Woods, p. 83.

13. Dreyfuss and Lawrence, p. 249.

14. *DeFunis* v. *Odegaard,* 416 U.S. 312 (1974).

15. Ibid.

Chapter 6

1. Joel Dreyfuss and Charles Lawrence III, *The Bakke Case: The Politics of Inequality* (New York: Harcourt Brace Jovanovich & Company, 1979), p. 38.

2. Ibid, p. 34.

3. Ibid, p. 41.

4. J. Harvie Wilkinson, *From Brown to Bakke: The Supreme Court & School Integration, 1954–1978* (New York, Oxford University Press, 1979), p. 54.

5. Dreyfuss and Lawrence, p. 46.

6. Wilkinson, p. 59.

7. Dreyfuss and Lawrence, p. 16.

8. Ibid., p. 15.

9. Ibid., p. 51.

10. Ibid.

11. Ibid., p. 46.

12. Ibid., p. 51.

13. Wilkinson, p. 267.

14. Ibid.

15. Dreyfuss and Lawrence, p. 43.

16. Ibid., p. 63.

17. Ibid., p. 74.

18. *DeFunis* v. *Odegaard,* 416 U.S. 312 (1974).

19. Dreyfuss and Lawrence, p. 89.

Chapter 7

1. Joel Dreyfuss and Charles Lawrence III, *The Bakke Case: The Politics of Inequality* (New York: Harcourt Brace Jovanovich & Company, 1979), pp. 173–174.

2. Ibid, p. 5.

3. J. Harvie Wilkinson, *From Brown to Bakke: The Supreme Court & School Integration, 1954–1978* (New York, Oxford University Press, 1979), p. 260.

4. Dreyfuss and Lawrence, pp. 166–167.

5. Ibid., pp. 176–177.

6. *University of California Regents* v. *Bakke,* 438 U.S. 265, 269–270 (1978).

7. Ibid.

8. Ibid.

9. Ibid.

10. Ibid.

11. Ibid.

12. Ibid.

13. Ibid.

14. Dreyfuss and Lawrence, pp. 191–192.

15. Ibid.

16. United States Constitution, Amendment XIV.

17. Dreyfuss and Lawrence, pp. 103–104.

18. Ibid., p. 194.

19. *University of California Regents* v. *Bakke,* Docket #76–811 Proceedings, p. 45.

20. Ibid.

21. Ibid., pp. 53–54.

22. Ibid., p. 54.

23. Ibid., p. 75.

24. Ibid., p. 61.

25. Ibid., p. 75.

26. Ibid., p. 58.

27. Ibid., p. 68.

28. Ibid., p. 59.

29. Ibid., p. 60.

30. Ibid., p. 73.

31. Ibid., p. 62.

32. Ibid., p. 64.

Chapter 8

1. "Bakke Wins, Quotas Lose," *Time,* July 10, 1978, p. 9.

2. Ibid.

3. "Middle Man," *Newsweek,* July 10, 1978, p. 29.

4. *Keyes* v. *School District No. 1, Denver, Colo.,* 413 U.S. 189 (1973).

5. Ibid.

6. 438 U.S. 265, 291 (1978).

7. Ibid, p. 295

8. Ibid, p. 310.

9. Ibid, p. 211.

10. Ibid, p. 314

11. Ibid., p. 212.

12. Ibid., p. 317.

13. Ibid., p. 328.

14. 42 U.S.C. 200d.

15. Bakke, p. 325.

16. Ibid., p. 327.

17. Ibid., p. 375.

18. Ibid., p. 379.

19. J. Harvie Wilkinson, *From Brown to Bakke: The Supreme Court & School Integration, 1954–1978* (New York: Oxford University Press, 1979), p. 302.

20. Bakke, p. 404.

21. Ibid., p. 407.

22. Ibid., p. 395.

23. Ibid., pp. 400–401.

24. Dreyfuss and Lawrence, p. 226.

Chapter 9

1. Joel Dreyfuss and Charles Lawrence III, *The Bakke Case: The Politics of Inequality* (New York: Harcourt Brace Jovanovich & Company, 1979), p. 226.

2. Ibid, pp. 226–227.

3. Ibid., p. 231.

4. *Steelworker* v. *Weber,* 443 U.S. 193 (1979).

5. *Fullilove* v. *Klutznick,* 448 U.S. 447 (1980).

6. Geraldine Woods, *Affirmative Action* (New York: Franklin Watts Inc., 1989), pp. 73–74.

7. Ibid.

8. *Fullilove* v. *Klutznick,* 448 U.S. 448 (1980).

9. Ibid.

10. *Richmond* v. *J.A. Croson C.,* 488 U.S. 469 (1989).

11. *Metro Broadcasting, Inc.,* v. *F.C.C.,* 497 U.S. 547 (1990).

12. *Adarand Constructors, Inc.* v. *Peña,* 652 U.S. 247 (1995).

13. Stephen Carter, *Reflections of an Affirmative Action Baby* (New York: Basic Books, 1991), p. 3.

14. Ibid., p. 88.

15. Nicolaus Mills, ed., *Debating Affirmative Action* (New York: Delta Publishing, Inc. 1994), pp. 214, 216.

16. Ibid., p. 46.

17. Ibid., p. 99.

Glossary

affirmative action—Programs that provide preferential treatment to members of social, racial, or ethnic groups that have been the victims of long-term discrimination. Groups most often included in affirmative action programs include African Americans, Hispanic Americans, Native Americans, women, Vietnam War veterans, and people with disabilities.

amicus curiae **brief**—"Friend of the court" brief; a brief filed by an individual or organization that has an interest in a case, although not directly involved in it.

attorney general—The nation's chief representative in legal matters and the legal advisor to the president.

brief—A written argument filed in court to support one's position.

compelling interest—A very important purpose.

compliance—Acting in accordance with a court ruling.

de facto segregation—Segregation that exists in reality, although it has not been created by law.

defense—In a legal case, the side being sued or accused.

desegregate—To do away with the segregation, or forced separation, of the races.

discrimination—A showing of prejudice in the treatment of members of racial, ethnic, or social groups.

equal protection clause—The clause in the Fourteenth Amendment that says that no state shall "deny to any person within its jurisdiction the equal protection of the laws."

minimal scrutiny—Lower standard for deciding whether a law passes the constitutional test; under minimal scrutiny any good reason for a law is sufficient to justify it.

oral argument—Presentation of a case in which one argues a point of view before the Court.

plaintiff—In a legal case, the party suing, or bringing the case before the court.

prosecution—The side that first institutes legal proceedings against someone in court.

quota—A number or percentage of people of a certain group that are chosen for a specific purpose.

rational basis test—The requirement that there be a legitimate purpose for a law that mandates different treatment for different groups of people.

reverse discrimination—Discrimination directed against members of a social, racial, or ethnic majority.

segregation—Forced separation of the races.

"separate but equal"—The policy established by *Plessy* v. *Ferguson* according to which separate facilities could legally be provided for members of different races, so long as they were of equal caliber. Unfortunately, they never really were equal in any way.

solicitor general—The presidential appointee who represents the executive department of the federal government before the Supreme Court.

strict scrutiny—The highest standard for deciding whether a law passes the rational basis test; under strict scrutiny, it must be shown that a law serves a compelling governmental purpose and that it is necessary to achieve that purpose.

swing vote—The vote that creates a majority of five when the Supreme Court is split with four Justices on one side of an issue and four on the other.

Further Reading

Belz, Herman. *Equality Transformed: A Quarter Century of Affirmative Action.* New Brunswick, N.J.: Transaction Publishers, 1991.

Dreyfuss, Joel, and Charles Lawrence III. *The Bakke Case: The Politics of Inequality.* New York: Harcourt Brace Jovanovich, 1979.

Dudley, William, and Charles Cozie. *Racism in America: Opposing Viewpoints.* San Diego: Greenhaven Press, 1991.

Gillam, Scott. *Discrimination: Prejudice in Action.* Springfield, N.J.: Enslow Publishers, Inc., 1995.

Hanmer, Trudy J. *Affirmative Action: Opportunity for All?* Hillside, N.J.: Enslow Publishers, Inc., 1993.

Lucas, Eileen. *Civil Rights: The Long Struggle.* Springfield, N.J.: Enslow Publishers, Inc., 1996.

McWhirter, Darien A. *The End of Affirmative Action: Where Do We Go From Here?* New York: Carol Publishing Group, 1996.

Mills, Nicolaus. *Debating Affirmative Action: Race, Gender, Ethnicity, and the Politics of Inclusion.* New York: Doubleday Dell, 1994.

Newman, Gerald and Eleanor Newman Layfield. *Racism: Divided by Color.* Springfield, N.J.: Enslow Publishers, Inc., 1995.

Patrick, John J. *The Young Oxford Companion to the Supreme Court of the United States.* New York: Oxford University Press, 1994.

Urofsky, Melvin I. *A Conflict of Rights: The Supreme Court and Affirmative Action.* New York: Scribner's Sons, 1991.

Wilkinson, J. Harvie. *From Brown to Bakke: The Supreme Court and School Integration: 1954-1978.* New York: Oxford University Press, 1979.

Woods, Geraldine. *Affirmative Action.* New York: Franklin Watts, Inc. 1989.

Index